MW00399581

In her book, *Jungle: A Journey to Peace, Purpose, and Freedom,* Cindy Henson takes us on a perilous journey as she flees her neatly packaged, corporate life in order to explore the tangled, untamed regions of her heart. Through her willingness to share each step of her physical, emotional, and spiritual journey, we see that we, too, can courageously confront our past and embark on a path of personal healing and professional transformation—to ultimately discover our true calling.

- Frances Fujii, Co-founder, CEO² and co-creator of *The Accidental CEO: A Leader's Journey from Ego to Purpose,* Boise, Idaho

Jungle: A Journey to Peace, Purpose, and Freedom provided me with the knowledge that most of us need to take this journey through reflection, suffering, owning one's struggles, and coming to a realization that one *is* strong. This book is powerful. Cindy Henson took me on a journey that wavered at times, yet always coming to the realization of the truth within her.

- Paula MacKinnon, Jungian Analyst, Boulder, Colorado

You may never leave home, suffer abuse, walk away from a "safe" corporate job, live in Costa Rica or attend the University for Peace. Whether you do these things or not, the unique and captivating story of one who did carries with it struggles, challenges, doubts, and triumphs we all face. Cindy's unique experience contains valuable lessons that you will need to preserve and succeed on your own journey to peace, purpose, and free-dom. These are the universal lessons we all need to know.

~ Len Elder, JD, DREI, CDEI,
Superior School of Real Estate, Charlotte, North Carolina

Cindy Henson's book, *Jungle: A Journey to Peace, Purpose, and Free-dom,* is an inspiring story of looking more closely at one's life and beliefs to find surrender and forgiveness at the core of next steps—things that are scary for so many of us, regardless of background or career choice. Her choices provide us with a timely example of how we can remember to broaden our perspective and find compassion, even for ourselves.

~ Molly Morrissey, Traditional Astrologer and
Guide for Your Sacred Pilgrimage, Taos, New Mexico

Jungle: A Journey to Peace, Purpose, and Freedom provided me with a different look into my own life and how I can simplify my busy life and do more things with purpose. Cindy Henson gave up what she knew was making her sick, for what she didn't know would make her better. She trusted herself and it paid off. Bold, surprising, raw, and wondrous.

~ Tracy Oberlies, Entrepreneur and Stylist, Ramona, California.

Jungle: A Journey to Peace, Purpose, and Freedom provided me with the desire to be even more fearless in my own life, to deeply question and reflect on my own actions. Cindy Henson's book is a compassionate, guided journey of courage and introspection. Humbling, honest, courageous, and inspiring.

~ Bruce Sindahl, Business Consultant, Boulder, Colorado

Jungle: A Journey to Peace, Purpose, and Freedom is a reminder of how important it is to stop and listen to our bodies—and really take the time to ask those hard questions: "Why?", "Is this where I'm supposed to be?", "Do I have the courage to change my life?". The answers are often scary, but Cindy's journey reminds us that getting what you want is rarely easy, is usually scary, but always worth it!

~ Jennie Rodrigues, Ramona, California

Take heart and inspiration from this courageous spiritual Bildungsroman that takes you on a journey from anytown, through blind corporate dedication, leaps to the jungle, then brings you truly home. You'll laugh, you'll cry, you'll learn something.

~ Loli Wescott, IT Administrator, San Diego, California

Cindy Henson's book lays clear all possibilities than we can behold if we just pay attention to our souls. A remarkable story on how we are sometimes brought to a complete halt in our lives so that we may truly begin again.

~ Paula R. Russell, Retired High Voltage Electrician, Supervisor, San Diego, California

An inspiring story of discovering one's inner peace, strength, and life's passion through self-acceptance, forgiveness, and love. Amazing!

~ Deb Gills, Retired Library Acquisitions Supervisor, Greensboro, North Carolina

JUNGLE

A JOURNEY TO PEACE, PURPOSE, AND FREEDOM

Cindy Henson

MOtivational PRESS®
LEADERS IN GLOBAL PUBLISHING

Published by Motivational Press, Inc.
1777 Aurora Road
Melbourne, Florida, 32935
www.MotivationalPress.com

Manufactured in the United States of America.

ISBN: 978-1-62865-510-0

CONTENTS

Disclaimer: This is a work of nonfiction. All the events in this book happened. Some names and identifying details have been changed in order to protect the privacy of the various individuals involved. The author has attempted to render the experiences detailed herein as faithfully as possible. The depiction of personal interactions are from the author's perspective.

To Dana—Your laughter, adventure, generosity, and love have turned my world from black and white to Technicolor. Thank you for seeing me long before I could see myself. You are the love of my life, woman of my dreams, and girl of my list. I love and cherish you and our partnership.

Deb and Pam—The best sisters anyone could ever have. My heart is overflowing with love for both of you.

To Bobbie and Harlan—Thank you for the gift of life. I know you did your very best for us. I love you!

To Danny Becerra—Thank you for bringing me love and encouragement when I needed it most.

Foreword

At forty-five, on the surface, Cindy Henson was living the California Dream. She had a beautiful home, shared with her life partner, a top position in a major firm, a high six-figure income, a religious base in the local New Thought church, and many devoted friends. Her free time was an ongoing exploration of the world's exotic sights.

However, her success in San Diego corporate Information Technology (IT) management was killing her. After a frightening faint in her workplace elevator, she was yanked into a new consciousness. Exhausted and ailing from a mysterious illness, Cindy discovered that she could no longer project manage her way through life. Logic and reason no longer worked. The stage was set for a midlife review that demanded she either make changes or perish from the life she worked so hard to create.

Cindy is like many in the corporate world, who lose sight of the purpose of their efforts—or didn't have a vision in the first place. Then life provided her with an opportunity—a wake-up call—to look closely at just how out of balance her life had become. She started first by reflecting upon the effects of a lifelong pattern of earning love and respect from family and colleagues by "taking one for the team," that nearly drove her to the grave. Her workaholic tendencies had her chasing love and approval in all the wrong places. She had to first learn to love herself before she could not only find balance in her work life—but more importantly save herself from a life-threatening illness. Cindy soon discovered that there was another way to do business in the world. After a year-long journey, she began to consider that people and our planet were just as important as profits.

If you're looking for a guiding light out of a life of overwork and overwhelm, read on.

Jungle: A Journey to Peace, Purpose, and Freedom is Cindy Henson's contribution to making right what has long been wrong in the world. Her story is unique yet her goals and achievements are universal. Her life and her journey will be an inspiration for so many people who find themselves "soul sick."

Make Cindy's story of courage, conviction, and commitment to making this world a better place for all, your own story.

~ Anita Sanchez, PhD, Founder of Sanchez Tennis & Associates, international best-selling author whose latest book is *The Four Sacred Gifts: Indigenous Wisdom for Modern Times.*

PREFACE

To quote John Lennon, "Life is what happens while you are busy making other plans."

Like many of us, I had a plan for my life, and I managed life like a business—with logic, reason, and goals that I could achieve and check off my list. I had my eyes set on retiring at fifty-five and with a very healthy 401k. My plan was to travel around the world and leave a legacy through my charitable works. To do that, meant I had to work hard and make the most money as fast as possible—no matter what the cost to my body, mind, and spirit. In fact, I didn't even know there was a cost. I was racing to win!

While that plan worked for a time, I was unable to sustain it. Working long hours, day in and day out, year after year, taxed me in ways I didn't foresee. A health crisis forced me to face some very difficult truths about my life—and about the way I was attempting to *live* my life. The truths demanded my attention, and I could no longer ignore them by working 60-70-hour weeks and priding myself in wearing a badge of honor earned by my workaholic tendencies. When I was finally forced to look at the truth about my life, I saw some things that I was hoping to bury forever and which made me very uncomfortable. But I had to look.

As you read through the chapters, you'll probably see yourself in my shoes—facing a crisis either of health or perhaps relationship, and having to make some difficult decisions by looking to your past to discover how you got to where you are. Like Steve Jobs said, you can only connect the dots by looking backward. I connected plenty of dots that drove me back into my childhood and my parents' upbringing to understand why I was so driven to pursue my definition of success in my own way and on my own terms. This definition, I later discovered, was based more out of fear and earning the approval of others, than it was on my soul's true calling on the contributions I was to make on this planet.

Perhaps, if you're lucky, this book has landed in your hands just in time to avert a crisis. My hope is that you'll be able to take steps to remedy unhealthy patterns and reclaim a balanced, meaningful life that looks beyond the bottom line of profits to the triple bottom line of people, planet, and profits. This demands that you look at how your actions affect the people around you and our global playing field. Equally important is claiming responsibility for your own health and well-being in body, mind, and spirit.

As you travel with me through my health crisis and into the rainforests of Costa Rica and the United Nations University for Peace—and my reinvention back into the world—my stories will challenge you to contemplate and engage in the following concepts—7 Principles to Peace, Purpose & Freedom.

1. **Tap into Your Fun Quotient!** When we set our intentions on having fun, even the most difficult situations and tasks can be much more enjoyable. When one person is determined to have fun, others often join in. So, smile, laugh, and have a good time—wherever life takes you. Life, and especially work, can be joyful and adventurous—and more rewarding in a joyful environment.

2. **Resolve Past Issues and Release Your Brain Power!** If upon examination, there is something from the past that is unduly influencing the present, it's vital to give it the attention required to

dissolve its power over us. Engaging in the practice of forgiveness and compassion assists us in doing so, and we put ourselves back into the driver's seat of our life. We move from reaction out of fear and anger to heart-centered responsiveness. Perhaps most importantly, making peace with the past allows us to understand that our situations do not define us.

3. **Discover what Juices You—and Pursue It!** Life becomes much more meaningful and enjoyable when we are engaged in activities that are important to us. It brings focus and clarity to our priorities. We know when to say "yes" and more importantly, when to say "no" to requests made of us. By inquiring of ourselves the source of a smile, a jig down a hallway, and a belly laugh, and what fills our well, and what brings us ultimate joy, we find our North Star, which keeps us on course as we discover and live our life's purpose.

4. **Activate Your Learning Gene!** Keep abreast of new ideas and share them. New discoveries are happening every day and many can improve our health, our mindset, our relationships, and our career. Read daily. Step outside your wheelhouse and be curious about what's happening in the world outside your own circle. Travel to exotic places. Share and debate new ideas until you have a full understanding of them. Keep what's important to you. Recycle the rest.

5. **See Your Colleagues Bigger than They See Themselves!** Learn to see the best in others and help them identify with and claim their untapped potential. Everyone needs a cheerleader now and then, a witness to their goodness and their talents. This is how we make our relationships thrive. Focus on the good, and vow to improve what's not bringing out the greatness in those around you.

6. Move to Action! No one else can do what we do. Once we discover our passions, it's time to actively engage our unique personal gifts and talents. By not doing so, some piece of the puzzle is missing. Our active engagement, with consciousness and purpose, are necessary so that our world and humanity continually evolve. We are needed to steward our planet and our global cultures, to bring peace to our families, our businesses, and our nations—so that we leave the world better than we found it.

7. Choose to be Unstoppable! Once you tap into your passions, vow to have fun, and know that obstacles appear. They're not meant to stop us in our tracks. They are interesting messages telling us to try another way. Challenges help us build muscle to climb higher mountains, reach for those goals that are bigger than ourselves, and assist us in discovering our own greatness. Never give up!

So, if you're like 73% of the working population that is dissatisfied with your job, you've stopped jumping out of bed with vitality and excitement for a new day, and your livelihood is interfering with your "real" life, *Jungle: A Journey to Peace, Purpose, and Freedom* may hold the keys to a solution.

Come along with me on this journey. You may be closer than you think to making your career and your life, happier, more productive, and absolutely amazing.

Cindy Henson
San Diego, California
October 2017

CHAPTER 1

ENTERING A NEW REALITY

I WOKE WITH A START, as if forklifted from my dream. I blinked my eyes and surveyed the room. Everything felt alien. I was stunned to find myself alone. I had not slept alone since I set up a home with my partner, Dana.

A shiver rippled through me, though the temperature was in the eighties and extremely humid. A tiny monster with a horned head and a dozen hair-thin legs skittered across the ceiling, directly above me. I bolted upright, my heart pounding in my chest.

Within seconds, I remembered that I was where I had planned to be—where I was led to be—and in fact had spent considerable savings to have this experience. Nestled in my rented casita on the edge of one of the world's last remaining lush rain forests in Costa Rica, I had committed the next year to heal myself and earn a master's degree in International Peace and Conflict Studies from the United Nations University for Peace.

And as I retraced all the decisions that led me to this place, dawn was leeching out of the darkness outside my window. The three hundred bird species awoke and began to caw, tweet, and chirp to one another. Frogs croaked their mating calls. From further away, a wild animal, that I had yet to identify yowled—a bit unsettling and a far cry from the hum of traffic on the interstate near my home.

As I breathed in the humid air and became reacquainted with my reality, the gray dawn turned from grainy monotone to brilliant Technicolor. Through the window, I saw the deepest, most verdant jungle foliage, what the poet Dylan Thomas called "the green fuse of life."

I sighed, exhaling my relief. This was not a prison cell, after all, and Dana had not deserted me. This was just my first day of waking up to her absence—a planned absence, for the coming year where we would keep to a schedule of sporadic separations, while she maintained our other life—the life I had elected to leave behind in a far different landscape, under a different sky, in the dry heat of San Diego.

This new experience was jumpstarted the year before, by another startling return to consciousness. The first event occurred on what I had believed was an ordinary start to my work day.

The day had begun as my typical work day always did—wake up, dress in a tasteful Jones of New York pantsuit, grab a piece of fruit, gulp my coffee, and then drive to my office. I had been working for Computer Sciences Corporation (CSC) for three years, and half of that time as Director of Organizational Development. My current project was stressful to say the least. My colleague Jeff and I inherited a project that was over-budget and way behind schedule, and very few people were happy.

I stepped into the lobby, oblivious to anyone around me, lost in my thoughts of what I needed to accomplish that day, and well aware that I could be facing numerous explosive situations that demanded finesse and patience. On cue, much like Pavlov's dog, the ding of the bell, prompted me to step inside the empty elevator. As I extended my arm to press the button for the fourth floor, I struggled to keep my mind on business. My head was spinning, my stomach was suddenly nauseated, and then my vision went black.

I regained consciousness on the elevator floor, my laptop bag, wedged beside my head, caught in the elevator door, causing it to open and close.

The elevator buzzer was blaring incessantly as the door kept slamming into my computer case. I sat up, and then reached for the railing on the elevator wall, pulling myself upright. I smoothed my hand over my nice pantsuit and took a deep breath. I soldiered on. That was what I always did. My mantra, my moral code, was: "Keep going no matter what." It had served me well. I was not one to give in. Not now, not ever.

I picked up the laptop case and my purse, as the elevator rose to my office floor. When the door opened, I slowly took uncertain steps toward my office. I was light headed and fighting the urge to hurl what little breakfast I did have. *What was happening to me? A stroke? A heart attack?* For the most part, I was fit, albeit maybe a few pounds over my ideal weight. However, I was a healthy forty-five-year-old woman. Yet, the heart attack possibility gave me pause. I had long ago been discovered to have a congenital heart defect—an enlarged heart with a faulty valve, diagnosed as Atrial Septal Defect (ASD). *A hole in my heart.* When I was twenty years old that hole was surgically closed, and I had been fine ever since. But now I wondered whether my wellness was an illusion.

My mind whirled with worry.

I placed my computer bag on my desk and sat down in my chair. I was determined to get coffee and pretend nothing happened so that no one around me would be privy to my current state. That would give me time to do what I did best: find solutions to problems.

Then the rational Cindy filtered in, and I thought of those twenty-five-year-old sutures that had closed the hole in my heart. Long suppressed memories of the regular fainting spells that began in my early teens and lasted until that surgery returned to me, along with an image of a ripping suture in my chest. Just thinking about that possibility made me fear that blood could gush through my body, unrestrained. Sensibility reigned and I knew I had to take some action. So, I sought out Jeff, my trusted colleague and friend. I shuffled into his office, unsure of my footing. Panic was beginning to take hold of me.

Jeff was sitting behind his desk, already engrossed in the day's work. "Hey, Cindy." He looked up from his computer screen, and he gave me one of his classic smiles, which let loose his beautiful dimples.

"Jeff, I don't feel well and I am heading home," I said barely above a whisper.

With a look of concern that bordered on horror, Jeff stood behind his desk and came over to me. "Are you okay?" His blue eyes peered into me, and I feared he might see more than I was willing to let on.

I averted my gaze, not willing to show him just how frightened I was. "Just a little nauseous." I turned toward the door. "I will check in at the end of the day."

"Are you ok to drive home?" I sensed from the tone in his voice that he was worried—a state he rarely visited.

"I'll be fine."

Contact with Jeff gave me the courage to get to my car and deal with my personal problem, as he dealt with our project difficulties that day. We made a great team. I provided the intensity; he, as senior on the project, exuded a relaxed confidence that set the stage for "We can figure this out." He had eighteen years in the company and had seen it all. And even though we'd only worked together eight months by this time, we knew we had each other's backs.

I weaved back to my office and sat back down. My heart was pounding in my chest. *I hope I'll be fine.* After mustering all my strength again, I grabbed my computer bag and purse and retraced my steps to the elevator and then to the parking lot. I barely made it to my car. As I slid into the driver's seat, I rested my head on the steering wheel. Rational Cindy muscled in over the part of me that was really scared. My heart may have been created with a defect, but my mind has always been very capable, logical. Using my problem-solving skills was why I was so good at implementing computer systems. See the big picture, assemble the jigsaw puzzle, and figure out the next indicated step. The way you do anything is the way you do everything, and so I applied these skills to all areas of my life.

Wasn't this just another problem to solve? What were my options here? Drive the twenty miles home when I could not even see straight. And then what? Stay there alone, with a possible bursting hole in my heart? Call Dana, to come help me? She was working 100 miles away and it would take her at least two hours to get here. By then, I might be…

Just the thought made me see specks in the San Diego sunshine.

I raised my head and looked out over the dash of my car. There was a hospital right in front of me. *How many times had I driven past this hospital and never thought much of it?* Now it was a vision, a Holy Grail, and right across the street. I knew that if I could get to the emergency room entrance, I could get help.

Since I couldn't walk very well, I drove across the street to the hospital. Later, I realized how foolish that was, but that other part of me, the Cindy who maintained her cool and steadiness no matter what, stayed conscious and crossed the busy road without crashing and actually parked. I staggered into the ER and managed to gasp out to the admissions clerk: "I am not feeling well," as I handed him my driver's license and insurance card. Then, I leaned against the wall and everything went black again.

I awoke on a gurney, with beeping machines all around me. I was aware of attendants bustling at my sides. Under warm blankets, I was held separate from all the noise by my cozy cocoon. It felt so good.

"Hello, Cindy. You fainted." As I opened my eyes, I saw the compassionate, yet tired, expression of the ER doctor, a young man, in his thirties. With a calming voice, he asked me questions about the long "zipper" scar on my chest from surgery and started jotting notes on my medical chart as I described the elevator episode to him.

"You should have called 9-1-1," he said, while making additional notations.

I nodded and then I remembered Dana. "I need to call my partner, Dana. Her number is on my cell phone."

A nurse brought the phone to me, and when Dana answered, I shared what I could as confidently as possible. After an initial gasp, she assured me she was on her way. Relieved that she'd soon be by my side, I drifted off to sleep, yet conscious of what was happening around me and to me. The entire medical team was poking, prodding, and testing me in an attempt to figure out what had happened inside my body. And at this point, I really didn't care. I had surrendered to the seductive warm drowsiness; it just felt so good to rest. For a time, I set my responsibilities aside, knowing that there was little I could do about anything in my current condition.

The ER doctor returned to say my heart, brain, and lungs all seemed to be functioning normally. There were no sprung sutures. What he meant of course was that there did not seem to be anything so urgent that was going to kill me that day or the next, so I would need to leave the ER so they could have my bed and tend to another person who required the immediate attention of the medical staff. While I really didn't want to leave my cozy cocoon, it was a relief to know that my heart sutures had not popped open.

When she arrived, Dana's beautiful face was etched with concern, her dark brows knitted together, and her brown eyes were liquid with fear. After she received the current synopsis of the situation, she took charge and phoned Jeff to let him know I would not be to work for a few days.

We didn't know at that time that it would be much longer—if I returned to work, at all. We thought we were dealing with an incident not a crisis that would demand more than rest, fluids, and hot foods and a barrage of follow-up doctor appointments.

As Churchill said during World War II, "This isn't the end of the war, but the end of the beginning."

This war was huge and had begun long before I was born.

Dear Reader,

Often when we are entering a new reality, we can be at odds either with ourselves or with people around us because many of us want to stay with what is known rather than try what's new. That might cause either an external war or an internal war. I invite you to take some time to contemplate the following:

- *Where might there be a war going on in your life? Is it external or internal or both?*
- *What is perhaps coming to an end?*
- *How can you look upon that situation as a new beginning?*

CHAPTER 2

PROJECT MANAGING MY LIFE

MANAGEMENT GURU Peter Drucker said, "You can't improve what you can't measure." I had heeded this advice during my highly successful, albeit very exhausting career, and I had always found a solution. It took good problem-solving skills and tenacity, but a solution was always attainable. I decided the solution to my current situation lived within the information and knowledge of the medical specialists I was to see over the next few weeks.

MBA school taught us that the first activity for any project was to prepare and organize all information into a file for fingertip access to the reports and schedules. To not prepare would leave me awash in mounds of paperwork. I had to handle this, as I would my business, or risk the label: Bad Manager. *And then what? Get sicker? Die?* My survival depended on my usual strategic and project management skills.

That was how the sojourn from illness to wellness began. In between resting and taking hot drinks and food, I prepared a three-inch binder, adding dividers by specialty: endocrinology, cardiology, neurology, and miscellaneous, for those unknown specialties that could arise. I proceeded to hole-punch the pages of medical reports that I had already been given and carefully filed them in the medical binder. I just knew the answer to my elevator episode was amidst the chaos of medical jargon on these pages.

As there were so many doctor appointments to be made and schedules to be kept, double booking could be an issue, I reasoned. I printed a blank calendar for recording the many appointments in an attempt to avoid the unproductive confusion that could occur in managing across specialists. I knew that if I managed this project well, I would get back to my familiar and comfortable life. The better I was at these organizing and managing tasks, the sooner I would reach my number one goal of getting back to work.

While I knew how to get things done, what I didn't know was how difficult it was to navigate the healthcare system. As it turned out, the specialists were taking appointments about four weeks out. I figured this did not really apply to me as I had urgent needs, and I would somehow be slipped to the front of the line. However, I did not take into account the "Attila the Hun" appointment schedulers, who were the gatekeepers to my salvation. With them, I needed to exercise my best methods of getting people to do what I requested, if I was going to be seen by specialists sooner than a month or more down the road.

While some of my business colleagues relied on throwing tantrums, I had developed well-honed methods to solve seemingly intractable issues in business. It made sense that my tactics would work with my current problem. There had to be a way to go over, under, around, or through the obstacles to get what I wanted. It was time to patiently (no pun intended) use my best methods with Attila. I jumped into action and tried the following:

The urgent-schedule method: "You don't really understand. I need to get back to work right away. My project is going live in two weeks, it impacts 20,000 people, and I lead it!"

In her best monotone voice, the receptionist said, "I am sorry, but this is the best date I can give you." She was not at all interested in my predicament. She had a schedule to keep and a doctor to protect from crazy and pushy patients.

The let's-try-another-way method: "Is there another doctor I can see in your office?"

She sighed and said, "No, I am sorry. The date I gave you is the earliest date available across the entire medical practice." I could tell she really wanted to hang up on me, but somebody had told her that hanging up on patients was unprofessional. She, instead, kind of listened through her well-positioned sighs and exasperated breaths.

My best and final method, *Then let me enroll you in solving my problem method*: "Is there a way to see the doctor sooner?" I asked.

"Only through a cancellation. And, you have to stay near your phone to receive the call when a cancellation occurs or I just call the next person on the list." She explained the alternative scheduling procedure that placed her squarely in her bureaucratic glory.

I really couldn't believe this. First my body gives out at a very inopportune time and now the guardian of all top-secret medical advice was strong-arming me!

"I will stay right next to my phone," I found myself lying.

While imminent death had been ruled out, I truly did need to discover what was going on before I went back to work. I didn't want to abandon my colleagues, or embarrass myself, if I had another untimely event. That would just be irresponsible. Not to say dangerous. And I needed to get back to work very soon.

Was it too much to ask to get in to see a doctor?

That thought carried through to my next call to the office. Keeping my colleagues informed of my progress—or lack thereof—was essential as the leader of the project. I diligently described the inefficient health care system and how I was not able to determine my prognosis because they had not yet determined my diagnosis. My plight was acceptable. Everyone had experienced or knew somebody who had experienced the same scheduling issue. I was caught in the limbo of the inefficient health-care system, and yet, it just wasn't right.

My frustration was rising, which only added to my fatigue—something I hadn't allowed to stop me prior to the elevator incident. In fact, I was quite proud of the stamina, productivity, and efficiency I possessed. I had always led a full life, and I told myself I really didn't need much sleep because there were always things to do, places to go, and people to see. Time was a wastin' if I wasn't on the move. Now, however, rather than maneuvering through my days on five to six hours of sleep, I was now in Sleeping Beauty land for twelve to fourteen hours.

During the call to the office, a decision was made that I be placed on disability with an undetermined return-to-work date. While I was not thrilled, I was relieved that I could now rest without milestones and a designated return date. I didn't yet notice, nor interpret, my relief as a signal that things might not be right in my life. This was much too early in my awakening to realize that when people and circumstances did not bend to my will there could be many other pathways forward than those I knew so well. Yet, the concept of allowing life to unfold was not even a remote thought in my mind.

There is a saying that, "The fish cannot see the water." Water is the very context in which the fish exists. It's all it knows. So, it is with people. The context in which we exist cannot easily be seen. And I, essentially, was a fish.

Dear Reader,

We often rely on the same skillset or tools in multiple situations. To use an analogy, we may choose a hammer when a screwdriver is more appropriate. We tend to use what we always know works.

- *Where might you be a fish in water?*
- *Is there a situation in your life that is calling for you to engage a new approach?*
- *What are you pretending not to know?*

CHAPTER 3

QUESTIONING MY REALITY

AFTER THREE MONTHS of rest, hot foods, and extraordinary efforts in project managing my health care and visits to the myriad of medical specialists, no one had a definitive answer as to what was ailing me. All they could agree on was that "it" was serious and my life was in danger. If not for Dana's love and care, I am sure I would have died during that time.

We had been together for five years, having met through mutual friends. In many ways, we were polar opposites. Dana was devoted to the public good; I was Big Business. Over time, however, she expanded my awareness of world issues—such as poverty that I had experienced—and ignorance and violence—with which I was also intimately familiar. And she shared her idealistic belief that these ills could be alleviated through public service. Dana believed local government could set the table with education, public infrastructure, and land-use, as well as environmental and governmental regulations to ultimately serve the public good. This was quite the opposite of my focus on the profitability of business.

The only knowledge I had about government was through my high school civics class. The courses within my MBA did not discuss the workings and purpose of a government, except to explain why government regulation was viewed as interference to those trying to run businesses and produce needed goods and services to the marketplace.

Our early discussions were often a clash of pro-government and pro-business value systems. We spent hours describing and arguing the best scenario of our own viewpoint, while bringing out the worst scenario in the other's viewpoint. While we had heated debates about laws, regulation, labor unions, monopolies, and greed of corporate moguls, we respected each other's career choices and knew that we were working hard at living our own values and beliefs.

We both worked long hours and taught night school at local universities. We played equally hard and made sure we had regularly scheduled vacations that involved hiking, backpacking, rafting, or cycling. We did frequent faraway fundraisers, including a trek in Africa to raise funds for an AIDS vaccine. We also cycled from San Francisco to Los Angeles, pumping the pedals to help AIDS patients in California.

Before Dana and I became a couple, I had done minimal international travel and knew little beyond the confines of the United States. In contrast, prior to our relationship, Dana had trekked in Nepal, participated in governmental information exchanges in Brazil, and vacationed in Mexico, Costa Rica, and Panama. As we began traveling together to international destinations, my eyes began to open more fully to see the world at large. Visiting developing countries such as South Africa, Zimbabwe, and Brazil exposed me to new ideas, which at the time seeded my interest in pursuing a different way to do business in the world. In a sense, these journeys were previews to the ultimate one I would take to save my own life.

We were constantly learning from one another, asking and answering questions. But now, there were new questions, and we were no longer quite equal partners physically. Dana was well, and I was nearly immobilized with a mystery disease that could yet kill me. The new questions could not be answered by simply looking at the physical body as something to be managed within the traditional medical model. The questions demanded that I explore the mind-body and spiritual-body connections. Initially, I resisted going to the new territories, relying on what I knew in the past to be true: our bodies are best managed through the healthcare system. Yet, this was no longer working. So, I did what most of us do when what we've always known to work no longer does: I surrendered and asked the deeper questions, the ones I would never ask when life is marching along.

It took courage and an open mind to consider: *What if physical ailments were not something to overcome? What if my body was giving me a message about my life? What would happen if I stopped battling life and began dancing with the possibilities this new condition presented? What if my life was supposed to take a sharp right, a detour from the straightaway of Big Business and the world of information technology?*

The latter is what concerned me the most. Big business was all I'd ever known and I reveled it—or at least I thought I did.

Working at CSC had been an enjoyable challenge for me. The company was an IT outsourcer with a strong value proposition: "Your IT headaches become ours, and we will provide all your IT services cheaper than you can provide them for yourselves. You just need to give us your hardware, software, networks, vendor contracts, and IT employees."

This proposition was very attractive for large businesses and large government agencies that saw IT problems as a distraction and IT itself as a necessary evil to their business, but not part of their core business. For me, going from General Dynamics, where I had been for nearly two decades, to CSC was a good career move that would give me opportunity to work with individuals in career changes through acquisitions and mergers. I was primarily responsible for onboarding employees and assisting them through the transition from their former companies to

CSC. Most of them did not embrace the changes that were happening *to them*. However, I saw the upside—and helped them see that the changes could enhance their career growth and income, and perhaps lead to more meaningful responsibilities. It was through building rapport and relationships with onboarding employees from our client businesses that I had the opportunity to work on high-profile IT projects that were not going well.

Prior to my health crisis, CSC had a $27M firm-fixed price contract to replace all financial and human resource systems for the County of San Diego. This was a very big deal. Jeff and I were brought in to right the ship that our predecessors had worked on for two years, spending nearly $27M, and had yet to deliver anything. "Contentious" doesn't begin to describe how high the emotions were running within and across the client group and our technology team. The client relationship was at an all-time low, with almost everyone having a blatant disregard for everyone else as experts, let alone as human beings. And worse, there was no clear path about how to change the situation, implement the systems, and repair the relationship between CSC and the County of San Diego.

Jeff and I began by assessing our team members and who we would need to replace to move from the blame game and despair to a "can-do" attitude. We asked the new project manager on the County side to do the same with her team. Then we asked the executives from both organizations to give us thirty days to evaluate the situation, create our new team, and share our road map and plan to implement the contracted systems. To their credit, they gave us the time and space to do just that. A new implementation plan was put into place with our new teams, and we began systematically implementing modules in a six-phase approach that was slated to take nearly two years to complete. The expectation to perform, work long hours, and give every ounce of energy to the promise that we had made was enormous. And we did it willingly.

Now, however, I questioned whether the long hours and pressure to get the job done taxed my body more than I realized. In fact, I began wondering if how I'd been working for most of my life was the root cause of my illness. I loved a good challenge and I loved the recognition of a job well done. However, was the payoff worth the toll it had taken on me personally?

Dear Reader,

It takes courage to admit that some things aren't working as well as they could be. The first step is admitting and then owning where we are overly invested, particularly when we've worked hard for something. This creates the situation where it becomes difficult to question that "it" may not be where we need to be.

- *Where might you be working too hard at the expense of some area of your life outside of business?*
- *What is the payoff that you are looking for?*
- *What circumstances in your life might be leading you to make a sharp-right turn in your career path?*

CHAPTER 4

IN THE BEGINNING

MY LINEAGE HELD little hope that I'd do anything to "get above my raising." I was born in 1958, the firstborn of a young couple—teenage bride Bobbie Crocker and her then twenty-one-year old Navy man, Harlan Henson. Rumor has it that Bobbie dated Harlan off and on through high school, even though she had another steady boyfriend, Doug. However, after a fight with Doug, Bobbie married Harlan at Christmas break of her senior year, 1955. Fresh off the farm, in Summertown, Tennessee, working odd jobs with an eighth-grade education, Harlan joined the Navy to support himself and his wife. Bobbie would say later that Harlan was so handsome she could not resist his marriage proposal.

Bobbie's mom, Lillian Crocker, was a hard-working entrepreneur, who owned a neighborhood grocery store and cleaners along with her husband, Julian. He had suffered a disability at his brickyard job and lost one arm to just above the elbow and one to just above the wrist. My grandparents worked long hours to make ends meet in the segregated small town of Columbus, Mississippi, during the fifties and sixties.

Harlan's dad, Clarence, was a farmer who transitioned to carpentry at a local factory when Harlan and his twelve brothers and sisters could manage the farm before and after school. Velma, Harlan's mom, was married to Clarence at fifteen and gave birth every other year for the next twenty-five years. Clarence was a strict disciplinarian, doling out switches on the back, butts, and legs that progressed to battering with 2x4s when the kids got sassy. This was the greatest legacy he passed down to his family—and one that I was privy to on far too many occasions.

Much of Bobbie and Harlan's child-rearing differences stemmed from Bobbie being an only child and Harlan having twelve siblings. They had different approaches. Bobbie's too soft for Harlan. Harlan's too vicious for Bobbie. The kids got caught in the crossfire—and I bore the brunt of the family legacy. Yet, I adored my father and have strong memories of Dad from my infancy. He was my hero. I was his precious baby girl, and he called me "Doll."

As I lay in bed, recuperating from my hard-to-diagnose illness, convinced that the rest of the world was well and at work, my first memory surfaced, unbidden. I was two years old and in a rolling crib that I managed to propel to the window, where I stood on tippy toes to watch for my hero to come home. I was so anxious to see him return that I would gnaw on the windowsill, filling my mouth with splinters. I soon learned that my father was far from a hero.

Growing up in San Diego in the 1970s, my life revolved around the military and a focus on the Vietnam war. My worldview was colored red-white-and-blue. My dad and all my friends' fathers were serving in the United States Navy. For six months out of every year, our dads were on ships deployed to Vietnam and the surrounding regions to protect our freedoms against the bad guys in the Soviet Union, Vietnam, Cuba, and any other communist nation that, given a chance, would annihilate us. You were either with the U.S. or you were against us. There was never room for shades of grey.

The overt and covert cues in our homes and our schools were about patriotism, freedoms, and working hard. My father often railed about his duty to go halfway around the world to save the "gooks" because "I'm protecting our freedoms," he'd say, often slamming his fist on the table. "This is what I signed up for. This is what I do. And those protestors! Damn hippies, degrading our country." From his frequent rants, I learned the difference between good and bad people. There was neither room, nor need, to have a different viewpoint. These patriotic military views soaked into my consciousness, and it wasn't until much later that I recognized that this was a rather simplistic explanation of the foreign and domestic policy of our nation. At the time, I felt so lucky to be born in the right country with the other God-fearing Americans. I bought into the idea that playing offense rather than defense was smart and necessary if we were all going to grow up safe and free. I believed "we" were right and that any war the United States entered was for a just cause and God was on our side in this battle.

The memories continued—the good, the bad, and the ugly. And there was a lot more ugly than I wanted to remember. Sister Deb was born at Balboa Navy Hospital in San Diego in 1960. I don't remember her birth, but I do remember the fight when Dad came home from deployment and found Mom was pregnant with Pam, born in 1961. He was adamant that this child could not be his, a rant he continued after Pam was born because she had dark eyes, dark complexion, and black hair in ringlets. Both Deb and I had blonde hair and blue eyes. His accusations centered on his distorted belief that Mom had slept with someone who had dark skin and dark eyes. As time went on, all of us started looking more alike and the timing of mom's pregnancy was no longer questioned.

My strongest memory was when we moved into a house, and my dad began to drink a lot. I recalled the scent of booze on him, when he lifted me up. I still longed to be near him, and I did outdoor chores so we could be together. Outdoors was safe. Inside, anything could happen, and it did. There was just too much hollering and hitting.

Dad's praise was paramount to my self-esteem. I loved to learn and did well in school. The only "C" I received in grammar school was in writing because it required practice and I didn't want to practice. He made me sit and practice writing my alphabet over and over. I hated it. Yet, I knew better than to get in trouble, or else there would be hell to pay.

And I did get in trouble just once. One afternoon in fourth grade, Miss Dowling asked us to take out our science book. When I looked over at Willie James, I saw he was struggling to get the book out of his desk. I noticed that he had spilled a grape Kool-Aid packet all over the inside of his desk and everything was stuck together in a purple sticky mass.

Willie was a chubby boy who barely fit in his desk. He kept pulling the book, and his desk began to jostle out of the row alignment. He and the desk fell over, like the TV show *Laugh-In* guy on the tricycle, and then Willie raised up his torn-up science book in victory. The teacher and the rest of the class rushed over to make sure Willie was all right, while I laughed hysterically. Regarding my laughter in poor taste, Miss Dowling told me I had to write, "I will not laugh in class" 500 times and turn it in the next day.

Being a smart aleck, I wrote, "I will not laugh in class 500 times." Not amused, Ms. Dowling sent me home to write "I will not laugh in class" line by line, a thousand times, and have it signed by a parent. It was due the next day. It took me all night to complete the assignment, and I wasn't feeling so jolly when I had to explain the assignment and ask for my mom's signature, begging her not to tell Dad. She signed it with an admonishment to stay out of trouble. I saw what happened when Mom made Dad mad. She got a black eye—and I was afraid that would happen to me.

As a nine-year-old, I soon grew to hate my dad and began to see my mom as weak-willed. She became a non-player for me and I just did what I needed to do to placate her, but I really wanted to please him. He was smart and held all the power—and that was something that I would remember well into adulthood.

His power over us was a regular occurrence. He accused my sisters and me of petty crimes, lining us up military style in our home. One night, he accused us of stealing a dime. "Who stole the dime off my dresser?" He dressed us down, yelling and drinking beer: We "sailors" had to shape up or pay the consequences. We were bad. We were thieves. "One of you stole *my* dime," he sneered, looking each of us in the eye. The stench of alcohol and cigarette smoke seeped from his breath.

Deb saved us and confessed, only because she had to go to the bathroom. I listened to the sound of her being beaten from the front porch. Vietnam was not only overseas, it was in our home, too.

There were other unspeakable punishments, and it wasn't long before I dreamed of escaping. As the eldest, I felt it was up to me to save my two younger sisters. I was in seventh grade, Deb in fifth, and Pam in third. I began to plot our escape, as only a twelve-year-old could; I imagined we would all flee together and hide in one of San Diego's deepest canyons. I devised a plan and even acquired an improvised modular home for us: a refrigerator box. One night after dinner, I invited my sisters to my room to share the plan. They were all in.

The next day I walked home through the canyon and realized my plan would never work. Mom and Dad would find us, and he would probably beat us even more. That night I broke the news to my sisters that we were not moving to the canyon.

The beatings and more had become so regular, and I had tired of taking one for the team, which I often did to protect my younger sisters, so I devised yet another plan. Plan B was to earn enough money to move out and take my sisters with me. I babysat in the neighborhood, afraid to ask for more than fifty cents per hour. I signed on as an Avon Lady and had a route where I would knock on doors to sell Avon products. It really sold itself. I made about $50 a month during that summer. I also began working evenings and weekends at my friend's parents' electronics factory. I saved every penny I made, and by the time Dad returned from his latest deployment, I had saved $700.

The common belief about war was that the communists were trying to take over the world, and to accomplish this they hurt and killed people to achieve their communistic goals. According to this definition, my dad was a communist. With this in mind, my fears had intensified into believing my mom, sisters, and I could be killed by my dad at any time. This only reinforced my desire to escape. So, I continued to study, work, and save as my only way out of this bizarre hellhole.

Essentially, my parents did not see eye-to-eye on anything—whether it was paying the bills to how the silverware was arranged in the kitchen drawer—to our dating. One night I was doing the dishes in the kitchen, while Deb and Pam were in their room studying. It was safer there.

Dad and Mom began yelling. I walked slowly into the living room feeling my heart quicken and my anger rise into my throat. Mom was slumped in a heap between the coffee table and the couch. Her chair was toppled onto its side. Dad was red-faced with the anger I was all too accustomed to seeing.

I quickly surmised what had happened, looking at the furniture and human wreckage. Dad had angrily gotten up from his brown tweed La-Z-Boy recliner, and jerked Mom out of her beige wingback chair, toppling it over. Then he had shoved her into the maple coffee table that caught her behind the knees, and she fell over backwards between the table and couch.

What is wrong with these people? I can't take much more of this bullshit!

I reached down and lifted Mom up, feeling her shaking in my grip as she stifled her sobs. I walked over to her toppled chair and turned it right side up. I boldly told her, "Go sit in your chair." She obediently did as I said, averting her gaze from my own.

I faced my dad and pointed my index finger directly at him, "She is getting back into her chair, and you need to sit down in your chair now. You both need to calm down and have your discussion reasonably. No more hitting!"

Marching back to the kitchen, I closed the pocket doors and turned up the music so I could no longer hear them. I felt strong and victorious in that moment. I even smiled, recalling their shocked faces.

I was nearly finished with the dishes and was about to make a mad dash to my bedroom to study when I heard them again. Something inside me snapped. I picked up a butcher knife, put it under a towel and walked slowly into the living room. I had already told myself, I would only use it if Mom was on the floor. I don't know why that was the requirement to not stab my dad—but it was.

As I entered the room, they were both in their chairs, pointing and yelling at each other. When they saw me, they stopped.

Dad said, "Look, Doll. We are in our chairs."

He had no idea that having his butt in that chair saved his life that night.

My victory was short lived.

We all knew that children were to be seen and not heard, and when their friends Jack and Betty arrived for drinks and cards one evening, we were introduced as the three perfect and polite daughters before we were exiled to our bedrooms for the evening. As I walked down the hall, I thought it all a bit strange, mainly because my parents didn't actually have friends. Jack was a shipmate of my dad's and they all believed it would be fun to get together. I, however, was worried. Drinking turned adult discussions into shouting matches in my experience, and I silently predicted tonight was going to be no exception.

Exile was appealing, and I was happy to be by myself, listening to my favorite album, Carole King's *Tapestry*. Through my headphones, music allowed me to drown out my crazy, loud, and unsafe world. Deb and Pam were playing games in their room. They were to go to bed by 10:00 p.m. and I could stay up until 11:00 p.m.

After I turned off my light, I slipped into sleep, thinking we'd all be safe for the night. Then BANG! I was awakened to yelling. "How dare you come onto my wife," Dad screamed.

"I am not coming onto your wife! I have my own," Jack shouted.

Over their voices, I could hear, Mom saying, "Calm down, honey," and Jack's wife was telling the men to stop yelling at each other. Then the screen door creaked open. From my window, I saw Dad hurl Jack out the front door while yelling, "Come into my house and put the moves on my woman, I'll teach you!" He slammed the door and stormed back into the living room.

Betty followed Jack to the car, and they drove off. No tire screeching. No honking horns. No yelling. *So that's what normal people do.*

By then the yelling had begun in the living room.

"You're nothing but a whore!" Dad raged.

Mom was crying and screaming, "I have never cheated on you. Calm down; you will wake up the girls."

Wow, Mom. Good one!

I'd had enough. I put on jeans, sweatshirt, and my sneakers. Walking with a fierce determination, I strode down the hall and right out the front door.

"There, I hope you are happy. Your oldest daughter just left the house because of you!" Mom shrieked.

"Oh, no she won't," I heard him roar, as I looked over my shoulder and began to run.

I should have been running from the start as he was still bigger, stronger, and faster than me; two blocks away from our house, he caught me by my hair. As he dragged me, back to the house, I began yelling, "Help me! Help me, someone!"

Winded from the sprint, he said, "Shut up. You will wake people up."

I just kept yelling, "Help me! Help Me!"

I didn't see any house lights go on, but I've no doubt the entire neighborhood heard my screams. They always heard the yelling at the Henson house. This was nothing new. What was new was that the fighting had moved out of my dad's domain into the street. But no one came to my aid.

When we came across our lawn, I could smell the dew on the grass and the light fragrance of the jasmine plants. I remembered thinking, *"You can't do anything to me at all that will hurt me or keep me down. It is a matter of time now before I make my move, you coward!"*

Dad dragged me into the living room and yelled two inches from my face, with his cigarette and alcohol breath assaulting my nostrils and saliva spewing onto my cheek, "You will never walk out on me again."

I very calmly said, "Watch me."

His first punch landed directly into my right eye. I flew backwards into the wall, cracking the outlet with the back of my head. I stood back up with my arms at my side and said, "You can't hurt me."

He came across the table at me again, wrestling me to the ground and punching me while I covered my face with my hands in a defensive posture. Mom was trying to pull him off me. Finally, he stopped like he had come out of a wild crazy place in his mind. He fell back into his La-Z-Boy, heaving heavily as he regained what composure he could possibly muster.

Rubbing my face splotched with tears and blood, I walked down the hall to my bedroom and locked the door, for the first time in my life. We had always been admonished to not lock the door for our own safety. How ironic. Our house was the most unsafe place in existence.

The next day, my face was so cut and bruised that anyone with any awareness of child abuse would know what had happened to me. Deb and Pam cried and hugged me when they first saw me. Mom said, "Let's put some ice on that." She scurried toward me with a dish towel filled with ice. I pushed her hand away.

"I am so sorry I hit you last night, Doll." Dad looked sheepishly over his coffee cup.

Really?

I ate my bacon and eggs in silence, avoiding eye contact with anyone. I was stoically winning my dad's crazy domination game and about to blow the cover of "the perfect family." And the next day, I went to school, even though they suggested I stay home sick. I had them right where I wanted them.

The only problem—no one even asked what had happened.

Dear Reader,

Principle #2 refers to "Resolve Past Issues and Release Your Brain Power." While we may believe that today is today and the past is in the past, there is a continuum between our past experiences and our current behaviors. There may be unresolved issues that unduly influence our life in the present. This either uses extra bandwidth in our brain or limits our creativity. Either way, our brains are not optimally performing.

- *Very often, our past holds clues as to what influences our behaviors. What memories or experiences do you have that may provide you with insights to your current situations?*
- *What situations still trigger a negative reaction?*
- *What positive memories arise from your past?*

CHAPTER 5

MY ROAD TO FREEDOM

WHEN I WAS SEVENTEEN, I learned about the effects of physical, emotional, and psychological abuse in my high school psychology class. I had long since vowed to avoid any experience I had with my father, refusing to be dominated ever again. I preferred the loving and gentle caresses of girls and had since eighth grade. There were never any power plays and no forcing of their will onto me, and no worry of condoms or pregnancy.

During one of the classes, we were asked to imagine the end of our life and write an epithet for our gravestone. I am certain this assignment was intended to be more about legacy and how we wanted to be known. But I wrote, "Cindy Henson March 19, 1958 – November 10, 1975. She worked hard."

Mr. Franklin, a middle-aged man with a bald head and kind green eyes, honed in on the death date, which was less than two months away. He asked me privately why I thought I might die soon. I told him I imagined a skiing accident where I fell off a mountain, doing what I loved to do. "Perhaps we can talk about this, when you're ready," he offered.

Mr. Franklin's questioning made me realize that I was scared all the time. I knew by then that Dad was not going to change. His drinking had escalated, and I began to believe his threats to kill Mom or me or all of us were real, and it was just a matter of time before one of us was dead.

I was also convinced that Mom would not, or could not, get us out of this situation. In hindsight, I know she was suffering from battered wife syndrome, a mental disorder that develops in victims of domestic violence as a result of serious, long-term abuse. Many times, I had asked her to divorce him. "We gotta get out of here, Mom," I pleaded.

She said, "I can't take care of us, honey. I don't have any money nor can I get a job that pays enough."

At last, one day, after a particularly bad rant and beating from Dad, Mom had had enough. We packed up and moved into a hotel room. Mom and I shared with Deb and Pam that we were not going back until Dad stopped hurting everyone. They revealed enough of their own horrors and admitted how frightened they were. They had been quiet to avoid further retaliations. I bawled because I thought I was protecting them by taking the brunt of his abuse. It was for naught.

The chaplain and the counselors eventually made Dad move out of our house, and we all went home. Yet, I knew I could not live in that house any longer and wanted to be an emancipated minor. Our counselor agreed, and my mom had no choice but to sign the papers. I was a senior in high school when I moved out. I had to finish high school, which I did while working at a factory. And even though I had received scholarships to go to college, I was too tired to bother at this point. I just wanted to work. I knew that working hard and saving money was my ticket to freedom.

Very early in my life, I found my refuge. At age fourteen, I was already in business—making and selling lanyards. In our suburban San Diego tract development house, our garage was to the uninitiated just a mix of yard tools, lawn mowers, old used furniture, and car cleaning compounds, but to me it was my money-making factory.

The parents of my high-school friend, Sandy See, owned an electronics factory. They were the perfect "Mom and Pop" business. Their four kids and their cousins all worked at the factory soldering circuit cards for medical devices. IVAC and IMED were two large medical device manufacturers in San Diego in the 1970s, and they contracted out their circuit card assembly to smaller factories around town that could produce them cheaper and more reliably than the main manufacturing factory.

Zig and Ruth were masters at getting production orders and needed to quickly find and hire people to fill them—"stuff" circuit cards with tiny resisters, diodes, and the newly invented integrated circuits (ICs) on the fiberglass boards and ready them for the wave solder machine. Their tiny factory of twenty people in a small industrial park in suburban San Diego always bustled with work and was always in need of help.

I spent a lot of time at Sandy's house, visiting with their entire family. Zig enjoyed his beer, much like my dad, only he usually just passed out. Ruth was similar to my mother, only she didn't put up with Zig's crap—and he knew it. Their house was safe, even with the similarities.

One Sunday, their entire family was in the living room cutting blue rubber cords to a specific length, and then crimping fasteners on each end. "What are you all making?" I asked them.

"Lanyards to hold the new electronic thermometers around the nurses' necks," Ruth said. She handed me the electronic thermometer sitting on the arm of the couch to show me how the lanyard popped into the plastic tabs on the side and held the rope so it could be placed around the neck. *This was so cool. I've never heard of an electronic thermometer.* I was so excited that I knew the people who were helping to build them.

As I observed them, I saw the inefficiency in their system and knew I could make them much faster than they were making them. "Why don't I make these lanyards for you?"

Zig hired me on the spot. He waved his hand across the stacks of two-foot diameter rolls of blue cord, dozens of small baggies of fasteners, and several crimper tools spread across the living room floor. "I will pay you a penny a piece for each cord you make. That includes cutting the cord to the right length, crimping the fasteners on each end, and placing them in bundles of one-hundred."

I quickly calculated that I could earn about $10 every weekend in my garage. "When do I get to start?" I excitedly asked.

"Now!" He started piling up the supplies. "Get all these materials out of here and take them home with you." He then sat back down in his recliner with his beer to watch the football game.

After Ruth dropped me off at home, I scanned my garage. With efficiency in mind, I decided to set up two operations. Cutting the cords the correct length was to be the first operation and then adding the fasteners was the second operation. I made a plywood table with sawhorses and marked the length required for the cords on the table with a pencil. I would grab the cord at the edge with my cutters, drag it to the black mark, and then cut the cord.

The spool behind me was rolling around and uncoiling into a bird's nest. I thought hard about what I needed to hold the spool in place and unroll at the same pace of my cutting. I spotted the leaf rake. *Perfect.* I placed the rake handle through the hole in the spool and taped the rake on two lawn chairs with duct tape. The spool could spin freely and unwind the cord at the same pace as I pulled the cord.

By the time I went to bed that night, I smiled to myself, convinced that I had come across a gold mine as I had already cut 1,000 pieces of cord. My back was a little sore, and I had a blister on my index finger and my thumb from squeezing the cutters, but nothing I couldn't adjust to in my first profitable enterprise. As I fell asleep, I thought through ways to crimp the fasteners in record time. There was money to be made and I was going to make it.

The next morning, I couldn't wait to get back to my makeshift factory. I wedged a block under the sawhorses so I didn't need to bend over as far. Band-Aid®'s protected my fingers from blistering. I found a roll of twine in the garage and used it to tie the cords in bundles of 100. After I had my ten bundles, I sat down in the lawn chair and I set up my fasteners in groups of 10 on the plywood workbench. I would always know how many cords were completed with fasteners and how many cords were remaining, at any point in time. This seemed more interesting than just having a pile of fasteners and not being able to discern my progress.

I measured out ¼ inch from the end of the cord and determined that the width of the crimper was a perfect template size to accurately get the ¼ inch every time. So, I created the most accurate and fastest process possible. I completed all thousand fasteners on both sides of the cord that day.

Sunday night, I proudly called Ruth and Zig to tell them I was ready for more supplies. I completed 1,000 cords for a $10 payment. At that rate, I would have $50 in the bank by the end of the month and be that much closer to my savings goal to leave home.

And perhaps best of all, Zig thought I was a rock star.

When I think about that now, I don't know whether to laugh or cry. I'm not sure whether I was working harder for the money or the approval. Back then it didn't matter. I had it all together, woven taut as a lanyard. And now, I was unraveling.

Dear Reader,

Unbeknownst to you, patterns have been created from your past experiences that have become a way of being in the world. However, with clarity about how our patterns were created, we can make changes. Consider the following:

- *Looking back over your life, what has been your primary motivator?*
- *How has love or money played a role?*
- *Whose approval have you been seeking?*

CHAPTER 6

QUESTIONING MY IDENTITY

B USINESS, EVEN WHEN it was troubled, was a safer place to be. I could organize it and solve issues. This was where I knew who I was and confidently made a difference—and I could be seen for my accomplishments.

Case in point: The largest private employer in San Diego was General Dynamics (GD). With 20,000 of the 100,000 employees in San Diego building cruise missiles and rocket ships, GD made tanks, fighter planes, and nuclear submarines in other parts of the United States. The company prided itself on being the one-stop-shop for war armaments. Anybody who was anybody worked at GD.

I began my eighteen-year employment with General Dynamics, and its subsequent acquired businesses, shortly after graduating with my undergraduate degree in Business with an emphasis in Management Information Systems at the age of twenty-five. I started in the information management department and was on the team that implemented the first electronic mail system at the Electronics Division of GD.

Unlike today, nobody, and I mean nobody, embraced technology or had a desire to change the way they did their work. The male, middle-aged vice presidents dismissed me with, "My letters and faxes work just fine. And honey, I don't type. That is why I have a secretary." Having always been smart about maneuvering my environment, I learned to navigate in the male-dominated war machine of GD. Being scrappy and twenty-five years old allowed me some latitude in trying out new ideas that were viewed by the executives as naïve and cute.

There was a significant life-changing benefit from my years at GD. I had an amazing opportunity, working for Dr. Terry Straeter, CEO of GDE Systems, and the divested electronics division of General Dynamics in the early 1990s. He was an inspired leader whom everyone wanted to follow. With a double PhD in Physics and Mathematics, Dr. Straeter cared deeply about people and especially the employees who worked in our company. He gave me the opportunity to transfer ten current employees onto a team for three years to create the needed culture change for GDE to understand the business at all levels of the organization. We no longer had a parent company performing corporate functions. We learned Total Quality Management (TQM) principles and how to eliminate waste through Six Sigma: engage front-line employees, use data to make decisions, effectively work in groups, and implement pushed-down decision making to the lowest possible level. Because we didn't have a corporate headquarters, learning this new culture was necessary for the 180 leaders of the 3,000-person organization because all levels of the organization were just ratcheted up a level when GDE was formed. The General Manager became the CEO, Directors became Vice Presidents, Managers became Directors, Supervisors became Managers, and Leads became Supervisors. We all needed to learn our new roles and embrace the job of the "Lean Team" to instill these skills in the organization, one project team at a time.

We studied texts on related subjects, attended seminars, and hosted conferences by leaders in the field—W. Edwards Deming, Peter Drucker, Peter Senge, and our mentor, Bill Lareau. During those years, we eliminated millions in waste, increased the maximum rate of production in the factory, and learned to work across the departmental silos. Our team of ten was inspired, engaged, committed, and we became the support scaffolding that helped GDE grow into an attractive acquisition for the next purchaser.

Fortuitously, this was the most personally fulfilling job in my corporate career, and in hindsight defined a way that I could contribute my learned skills with my natural talents to hone a successful management consulting practice twenty years later. This experience also further ingrained the "take it for the team," mentality that had provided a great deal of personal satisfaction, won the approval from others, and made me feel very valuable. The behavior pattern also was evidence of a lifelong pattern where I pushed my body to limits that were unhealthy.

Now, during my illness, the sad fact was that I didn't even know that I was tired! I wondered why I didn't know that my body needed to rest and rejuvenate, likely another example of a fish not able to see the water in which it swims. It was a blessing and a curse to possess a strong body, a strong mind, and a strong will. It had never occurred to me that just because I could go, go, go, did not mean I could defy the laws of nature and life itself, without consequence.

The consequences were something I explored in my first doctor's appointment with Dr. Endocrine. He was a nice man and clearly a mature doctor with tried and true ways to test and medicate for inefficiencies in my endocrine system. I thought he might be a diabetes doctor as my grandma had been treated by an endocrinologist for her diabetes. *Did I have diabetes?* I had something serious, and I wanted to give it a name. *Then it could be managed.*

He assured me that diabetes was not the culprit, and that he was much more than a diabetes doctor. However, he was concerned about my extremely low blood pressure (BP), of 85 over 60 and asked me to start taking salt pills. He also wanted me to take my blood pressure reading every morning and every night. I immediately recognized an opportunity to create an Excel spreadsheet and hand record my BP twice a day. "Cindy the Organizer, Creator of Systems," was on the case.

"Come back after your blood, urine, and saliva tests, and we will get you on the road to recovery," he said with conviction.

The next specialist I saw was the cardiologist. After explanations of the recent episode, of which I had crafted into a very articulate and short explanation, he asked me a slew of questions about my medical history as it pertained to my heart. He was most intrigued about my days of fainting between 13-20 years old. I interpreted this high level of interest as care for me, although I think he was more interested in the intricacies of the heart and the circulatory function. I believed we would have a diagnosis by the end of this appointment. Then I would take some pills and then back to work I would go!

He continued his questioning: "How often did these spells occur?"

"Generally monthly, although I didn't always fall down. I realized that sitting down putting my head between my legs when I felt nauseous would eliminate the dizziness and I could prevent the faint."

In my teens, my mom had taken me from doctor to doctor to find the root cause of these spells, but no doctor was that curious. They were busy, over scheduled and gave a simple yet plausible diagnosis each time, such as the stomach flu, a cold, sinus infection, bronchitis, and the ever popular, "It is just a young woman issue," with them adding, "She will outgrow it." They then would prescribe medicine, and I would leave to faint the next month.

The Atrial Septal Defect (ASD) was finally diagnosed while I was in the doctor's office one day for a case of bronchitis, when, with its characteristic sudden onset, I could feel that I was going to pass out. The doctor told me to let it happen and he would catch me. I awoke lying on the examination table. I was looking up at the doctor and nurse as they were looking down at me. He said, "This is not normal," and they immediately sent me to the hospital for tests.

Within the hour, the diagnosis was made and confirmed. The doctor pronounced it as he casually strolled into my hospital room, "The chest x-ray shows your heart is twice the size of a normal heart. Since the heart is a muscle, it has been working extraordinarily hard to pump blood to your brain and we suspect a hole that did not close at birth. We will schedule a cardiogram to determine the size of the hole so we know how to properly close it." Then he turned and left the room the way he entered it.

The cardiogram revealed a half-dollar sized hole that would require open-heart surgery to repair. This all seemed scary so I contemplated not having the surgery. Fortunately, the doctor convinced me that my heart would probably stop beating by the time I was in my late twenties if I didn't take action. Translation: If I did not have a surgical repair, I would be dead in a few years. Dying that young seemed tragic and unnecessary. I soldiered on through surgery and was discharged in five days. My mom stayed with me while I was in the hospital, and the first week at home she cared and cooked for me. True to my style, I was back to work within three weeks.

Now twenty years later, explaining my medical history, each and every time I went to another specialist, prompted me to further systematize the process. All I had to do was type up my story and point to the paragraphs that were pertinent for that specialist. That quick access information, along with my BP reports and the specific lab tests, should be everything that was needed for the experts to make their decisions, and I could get back to my real life. That was my plan, anyway. My entire life centered on finding a logical explanation for the elevator episode. Behavior is not arbitrary—I knew there was an answer out there and I was determined to find it.

There were still plenty of unanswered questions where my health was concerned. While I did not have the pressure of a time line to get back to work, I began to worry that my colleagues would just forget me while I was out on disability leave. The company legally had to give me a job when I returned, but I worried I'd be considered damaged goods and no longer the person to be counted upon. Belonging was critical to my very existence, as was being valued for my performance.

I had enjoyed a meteoric rise in business because I was smart and could learn fast, adapt to changes, and figure out the rules of whatever new game came along. Furthermore, I worked 60-70 hours a week, an "old school" employer's dream. I could be counted on to do whatever was necessary, within ethical and legal limits, to implement my projects. My early performance reviews went something like this, "We can count on you to always get projects done, on time and under budget, and you seem to be able to relate well to all the people involved; we just need you to keep learning the business."

It took me many years to realize that the businesses I worked in were so heavily weighted by financial results that doing a good job was important and working well with people was important, but short–term financial results meant everything. I was internally resistant to sacrificing good leadership, employee involvement, and excellent quality for financial results. They felt like a dichotomy to me during those years. I could not yet articulate my understanding of these concepts, but I believed in my soul that excellent financial results were in fact the *result* of good leadership, employee efforts, and quality products and services—not a dogged focus on the bottom line.

Looking back, I can see that they were probably not at all suggesting an either/or solution but a mix of the two. Of course, I didn't talk about my viewpoints for fear of being labeled a socialist. After all, everyone knows that capitalism is the true backbone of business.

As a result of not having the insights, skills, and tools I now have, I silenced my beliefs to fit in with the business guys. I somehow got the message that my viewpoints were less important and not as valued, so I kept quiet. Yet, most of them were great guys and driven by something different than what drove me.

However, being the good soldier, I began adding the short-term financial gains and downplaying any long-term results as part of my monthly and quarterly presentations when reporting out on my team's results. The respect and acknowledgement I received felt tenuous at best. *What if they found out I was a fraud and I really didn't believe in the same business procedures and rituals in which they believed?* This imposter syndrome was the basis of my fear that I would be forgotten while in medical disability land.

Meanwhile, I faithfully measured and recorded my blood pressure (BP) several times a day, as instructed. I was searching for trends. As we know from business school, data is only information when we have enough data points and can begin to see trends which can predict future performance. Since I didn't have my statistical process control (SPC) software on my home computer, I did a rudimentary SPC graph and discovered that the outliers and low BP occurred just as I was standing up from a sitting or prone position. If I would just stand up slowly, I could ensure I was not going to faint before taking a step forward.

I was convinced I had found the source of my fainting and all would soon be back to normal. I decided to complete all my tests ordered by the endocrinologist and cardiologists and bring this BP data to each of them for their expert opinion. With all my test results, my own BP measurements, the last twenty years of my medical history that I had finally received, I was quite pleased with my data and strong record keeping. I religiously carried the medical notebook to all appointments and could quickly get the data that any medical professional needed since I had tabbed the notebook.

In the follow-up appointment with the cardiologist, he determined that my data was telling him exactly what he needed to know. Most of my tests were normal, except for one heart measurement that indicated to him that I had a leaky heart valve that was not allowing the blood to flow properly. He wanted me to wear a Holter Monitor, a portable device that measured and relayed the results of my heart performance for a week.

I believed we were nearing the answer, and I would be on my way back to work in no time. I followed his instructions to the "T" and all data was sent, received, and analyzed by my next appointment, two weeks later. He diagnosed Postural Orthostatic Tachycardia Syndrome (POTS). In lay person's terms, each time I stood up from a sitting or lying position, my heart would race as though I just ran a marathon. Therefore, I felt tired and fainted each time I changed my position. According to the Mayo Clinic, this is a well-known syndrome, sometimes also called "The Orthostatic Intolerance Syndrome" (OI). POTS is a condition in which an excessively reduced volume of blood returns to the heart after an individual stands up from a lying down position. The primary symptom of OI is lightheadedness or fainting. In POTS, the lightheadedness or faint is also accompanied by a rapid increase in heartbeat of more than 30 beats per minute, or a heart rate that exceeds 120 beats per minute, within 10 minutes of rising. The faintness or lightheadedness of POTS is relieved by lying down again. Anyone at any age can develop POTS, but the majority of individuals affected (between 75 and 80 percent) are women between the ages of 15-50 years of age. Some women report an increase in episodes of POTS right before they menstruate, which made sense of the fainting spells in my teenaged years. POTS began to explain the elevator incident.

But now I had a whole new set of questions. *How did I get this condition? Is it curable? How do we proceed? What else might be going on?*

Dr. Cardio explained the sympathetic and parasympathetic nervous system and that I had a systemic reaction in my body that was preventing many of the healthy and normal body functions to work correctly—symptoms such as the eyes tearing, the mouth producing saliva, and the heart automatically responding to the level of exertion of the body. I realized that my eyes and mouth had been very dry since I had been out of work. I was concerned, but didn't know that it meant anything, so I hadn't reported it. He let me know that he did not yet know the cause of POTS and the heart valve issue. Consequently, he didn't know how to treat it, so he referred me to a neurologist to check out my nervous system.

In the meantime, I had faithfully completed all the tests ordered by the endocrinologist, and he was unable to diagnose anything except low blood pressure. After I told him about the POTS diagnosis, he released me from his care. He did, however, suggest I keep taking the salt pills to keep up my blood pressure in a resting state.

So off I trotted to Dr. Neuro, with my three-inch medical binder in hand. He asked a lot of questions for which I answered, usually with data from my notebook. After twenty minutes of questions and no physical exam, he told me I was depressed and gave me a prescription for Paxil.

Depressed? Are you kidding me?

"If you have been through what I have been through the last three months in this screwed up medical system with no pathway forward, you would be depressed, too!" I shrieked. "I came to you for your expert opinion on my nervous system and you cop out with a depression diagnosis! I am not taking depression medication because in my soul I know this is not the right diagnosis!" I stood up, wobbly, because I still couldn't stand up very fast without being dizzy, and with Dana holding my elbow for balance, I marched out of his office.

I cried the entire way home. "How dare he say that to me? This can't be the diagnosis after all this time! I was perfectly un-depressed before I fainted in the elevator! What is the problem with the medical community?" I vented to Dana as she maneuvered through traffic.

Dana and I discussed the medical system the entire drive home. We decided that there did not seem to be an advocate for me in the system, one that looked at the whole body. We concluded that the variety of specialists knew their individual specialties, but nobody looked holistically, across the various specialties. I felt so lost. We only had two diagnoses: POTS and a leaky heart valve and no answer about what to do next.

In the meantime, I was losing weight and still extremely fatigued even with sleeping twelve hours a day. I began to wonder what it would be like to slowly die because there was nothing that could be done for my physical body. I spent all my waking hours trying to solve my health issue and find a solution. My only other activity was to slowly walk around the block. Mainly, it was to get a change of scenery. We lived in the suburbs so I walked the same neighborhood each day.

After Dr. Neuro said I was depressed, I realized that I was definitely not happy with my current circumstances. I had worked professionally for twenty years and was by all standards very successful. To find myself a near invalid without a plan left me very unsettled. I began to question myself and my confidence waned.

Prior to the elevator experience, I believed that I knew myself and that I was living my life to the best of my ability. I also believed that I was connected to all sentient beings. My actions impacted others, and therefore, I had a responsibility to hold myself to high standards and conduct my life in a way with which I would be proud. This level of seriousness, responsibility, and personal significance was in part why I worked hard and had successfully made my life work to this point. I gave myself high marks on striving to do my best, and I was proud of myself—and my accomplishments, thus far. I did not dwell on the pain and injustice of my childhood. *What good could that do?*

Yet, it was from this place of hopelessness as I looked forward that had me wondering about what else life might be about. I asked myself, "If I was not a business executive, then who was I?"

Dear Reader,

We forget that we are not our identity and we are not our role. However, with clarity about how our patterns were created, we can make changes. Consider the following:

- *What role do you identify yourself with?*
- *Is this the entire truth of who you are?*
- *What do you fear others might discover about you?*

CHAPTER 7

AN ALTERNATIVE REALITY

S HEER UNADULTERATED TERROR bolted into my awareness. *"If I am not a business executive, then who am I?"* That thought floated into my consciousness like a big rain cloud on a spring day. My heartbeat quickened and pounded in my ears. My breath became shallow, and I felt like I was drowning in the ocean, gasping for air.

As I regained my composure, I convinced myself that answering that identity question was not really necessary. I rationalized that everyone had crazy thoughts all the time, but we didn't need to follow them into a black cloud of fear and despair. So, I locked the thought into a black box that I promised myself to never again open. Or so my thinking went at the time.

My daily habit was to take a slow walk around the block of my upscale neighborhood under the brilliant sunshine. Our area was beautiful—with the well-designed houses, well-manicured lawns, and colorful, lush flower beds. Our home was also an attractive centerpiece, a four-bedroom ranch with a large redwood deck that fit the area. Our backyard was a lush garden tended by Dana. Considering my origins, this house was a dream, and the neighborhood an oasis. But now, both served as my sanatorium. I was too ill and weak to leave.

During the day, there were only three types of people evident in this bedroom community—the gardeners and housekeepers who maintained the beauty and young parents or nannies pushing infants and toddlers in strollers. At midday, I might see telecommuters out for a jog to battle the fatigue of sitting at a computer for ten to twelve hours a day. I saw the same people with enough regularity to warrant a wave and a brief greeting each day: "How are you doing today?" Or, a more casual "Hi," or "Hey." Now, I wondered what they thought of me, as I had become this invalid orbiting the block.

On this day, I stopped at this especially beautifully shaped maple tree that I had driven or walked by for twenty years, without the honor of a simple glance. I was startled to see that tree was a vibrant green that glowed with an iridescence that radiated in Technicolor. It was as though for the last twenty years, I had been seeing the tree in black and white. This Technicolor phenomenon had only happened at one other time in my life: when my family bought our first new color television set. My mom, sisters, and I were all gathered in the living room in excited anticipation as my dad hooked up the antenna. When he turned the TV on, the color jumped right out of the screen. It was magical! For about a week, I failed to even follow the TV show plots because I was so enamored by the colors.

As I continued looking at the tree, I observed the shape of every leaf. I noted the delicacy of the veins, so perfectly symmetrical and repeated thousands of times in this tree. I traced how the leaf was connected to the branch in a recognizable pattern that was again repeated hundreds of times. The branches then formed the upward reaching shape of the tree. The branches were connected to the textured strips of bark that formed the tree trunk. Without even seeing the roots, I knew they existed and were doing their one and only job of creating a foundation, deep and wide, or the tree would topple over.

Awareness of physical time and space disappeared and was replaced with a calm sensation that washed over my entire body. I did not ever want to leave this spot and this magical and awe-inspired feeling. Eventually, I walked back to the house. I didn't remember anything I did for the rest of the day. The sensation, a state of being, was otherworldly. I didn't judge it, categorize it, or try to name it. I just let it be.

The next day on my walk, I stopped at the shining tree. Again, I simply observed the details and intricacies of the tree. I began to wonder when the tree was planted and how long it would live. I was so drawn to that tree that I stopped there for three successive days, and then, like the color television set, the magic eventually faded, and I got back to the plot of the TV show—in this case, my life.

However, unlike the plot of a TV show, I was transfused with a renewed connection to my Spirit. In these precious moments at the shining tree, my circumstances, health issues, and identity had fallen away. I had no worries, no cares, and no place to get to. It was glorious, and I felt a freedom I had never imagined possible.

My intellectual curiosity was now piqued by two inexplicable events. I had fainted in an elevator for no apparent reason, and now I had stood in front of a shining tree that transported me to a mystical place that defied my visible world of management, metrics, and logic.

Could it be that there was not a logical explanation for what had happened to my body in the elevator that day? Maybe there was a mystical explanation that was in the invisible world. But how was I to access it? Or perhaps, I have lost my mind. I don't know what to make of all of this.

My judgments and logical mind then kicked back in and I realized that I could not tell anyone other than Dana about my tree experience because they would think I had lost my mind. So, I continued my regular daily rituals as I awaited my next cardio appointment. My mom, family members, and friends visited and called me during these three months of convalescing. I shared the medical experiences and the current prognosis. Everyone was sympathetic and offered to assist in any way they could. I felt loved and completely baffled.

One Sunday, Dana and I attended the Sunday Celebration service in the New Thought Community in which we were members and I casually mentioned that I was having difficulty getting a prognosis for my POTS and leaky heart valve diagnosis.

One of our dear friends told us about a friend who had a health issue that seemed unsolvable by Western medicine. She had gone to an intuitive healer and was now feeling much better. Up until now, I had entertained alternative medicine techniques such as acupuncture, chiropractic, and massage for lower back pains and strains, and had good results. But I had never heard of an intuitive healer. Remembering the shining tree, I decided that while intuitive healing was something out of my logical comfort zone, the tried-and-true Western medicine doctors were seemingly at a dead end, so I should approach this healer without the skepticism that I normally possessed.

Dana made the appointment for later in the week—a stark contrast to the long waiting list to see someone in the mainstream medical field. The intuitive healer's office was less than one mile from our house. I was starting to believe that some force greater than my own logical thinking was controlling my destiny. I was hoping it was guiding me toward healing—and not my eventual demise. Yet, hope was difficult to maintain. I had never known such profound exhaustion and my spirits were at an all-time low. I was beginning to believe nothing would help me.

"I don't think this is going to help, Dana," I said when the time came to go to the appointment. This "give up now" attitude ran counter to my history; yet, I was also aware that it was a syndrome that would booby-trap me at key moments of my life, in my education, especially. A subversive attitude resided within me, which could stop me from taking positive action to better myself in many situations.

Dana was having none of it. "We're going. You can decide after this appointment if you want to continue." Her eyes held fear that she was going to lose this battle with me.

When we walked into the intuitive healer's office, my resistance continued as I began to fill out the millionth form that I had completed in the last three months. After about two minutes, I began to cry and gave the clipboard to Dana. "I am done with it all!" Refusing to allow me to succumb to my hopelessness, she completed my forms and turned in the clipboard to the very warm receptionist.

We waited only five minutes before the doctor came out and welcomed me to the office. Dr. Brett was of medium height, in his mid-forties, with dusty brown hair, who exuded an air of peaceful confidence. He had me lie down on the examination table and let me rest while he asked his questions. Dana answered most for me. I was beyond exhaustion and nodding in and out of my weakening state. He asked permission to touch me and began poking around my stomach. Then, he left the room and brought back several bottles, which I later learned were Chinese herbs, minerals, and vitamin supplements. He placed a bottle on my stomach and then alternately raised each of my arms and legs, telling me to resist his pressure, a technique called muscle testing. This went on for about ten minutes until he found what he was searching for. He then gave me a cup of water and a pill to swallow. He said he would be back in fifteen minutes and that I should just lie there and rest.

When he left the room, Dana shared a profound realization, "He's the first doctor who has actually touched your body."

All the other doctors and specialists had simply used the stethoscope to listen to my heart and lungs, and then they spent our time together reading test results. With them, I didn't have any satisfaction. However, about ten minutes after I took the pill, I noticed that there had been a subtle shift in my energy.

Dr. Brett came back and after checking in with me, proceeded to test some other remedies. Once again, he asked me to lie down and rest. "I'll be back in fifteen minutes," he said as he left the room.

After a few minutes, I sat up. "This is amazing," I shared with Dana. "I feel better than I have in months."

The process was repeated three more times, and each time my vitality improved. Dr. Brett spent a total of 2 ½ hours with me—another stark contrast to the fifteen-minute appointments with the mainstream medicine specialist. Prior to leaving the office, he gave me a Chinese herb, vitamin, and mineral regimen, asking me to come back in three days. He also reminded me to monitor how I felt after I took the regimen and be prepared to report back.

As we were driving home, Dana asked, "So what do you think?

I stared out the window at the sunlight dancing on the city skyline and said, "I'm beginning to have a glimpse of my old self, again." And with that I began to cry uncontrollably. Torrents of tears dripped down my cheeks. That was the moment that I regained hope that I might come back from this debilitating illness.

On some level, I knew that I was meant to do much more in my life, and my previous methods were inadequate for the journey that was ahead. If my illness could be alleviated by alternative medicine, there must be more, as yet unseen and unknown, for me to discover.

Dear Reader,

For those of us who are goal oriented, letting our hands off the wheel and surrendering to what is being presented by current circumstances can be unsettling. However, this provides an opportunity to reflect on how there may be different approaches to the way we're "managing" our lives.

- *Describe a time in your life where you were transported out of time and space—and life around you seemed more vibrant and alive.*
- *What might you be meant to do that goes beyond your current circumstances and belief system?*
- *What is the reason you might be resisting?*

CHAPTER 8

QUIETING THE MONKEY MIND

THESE NEW EXPERIENCES of feeling better some days, and still feeling rotten others, was a roller coaster in and of itself. I began reading new books, far outside my business and leadership wheelhouse, trying to understand more about myself and my place in the world. I recognized that my life, while successful, was maybe not the path that I wanted to be on anymore. It was difficult to admit this to myself because I didn't want to ask the questions. I was so afraid during this time. When I look back, I realize my identity was crumbling—one that had taken me a long time and a lot of effort to establish.

Identity is a powerful concept. It sets us up in our world. It becomes how we speak about ourselves and even how we introduce ourselves to others. "Hi, I am Cindy Henson, and I am an executive with such and such corporation." We actually talk about ourselves by our roles and what we do, not actually describing who we are. In that vernacular, I am a daughter, sister, partner, friend, colleague, executive, and neighbor.

We also talk about what we do, like attending a certain school, obtaining a particular degree, and working at a specific job in a business. While this is helpful to locate oneself in the geography of the world, it says nothing of who we are. In fact, it is not even close to who we really are. Our identity can be so woven into the fabric of our very nature such that we don't even see that it is simply a construct that we use to talk about ourselves, and yet another example of being a fish unable to see beyond the water.

The concept of asking myself, "If I am not this executive, then who am I?" continued to absolutely terrify me. I had no idea. Absolutely, no idea. None, nada, nein!

The only other time I experienced anything remotely like this was after the ending of a previous long-term relationship. As I was pushing my cart down the grocery aisles, I realized that I was selecting food that I had always selected when grocery shopping. I asked myself, "What did I want now that I could have anything that I wanted and did not need to cater to another's choices? My epiphany—I did not even know what food I liked or wanted. I walked out of the store, leaving my cart in the food aisle with somebody else's food choices. I sat in the car crying. *Wow... how can that be? Is it possible I don't really know what I like to eat?*

That was the only other time I had that kind of lost feeling. The mask I had been wearing was falling away with no real person or substance underneath.

So, who was I really?

The books about spirituality and our connection to the divine turned my thinking upside down. The idea that there was another me that was not the me I knew—that I could actually observe myself as I went about my day—that I could watch my thoughts and my emotions, observe my chatter inside my brain—was startling and hard to understand. I rejected much of what I read as crazy talk. It sounded very woo-woo, and I was not a woo-woo person. I followed logic, made decisions based on facts and rationality. These concepts, like the observer self, a power in the universe greater than myself, and creating one's own reality, could not be seen nor proven, so they could not possibly exist. *Or could they?*

I was also uncomfortably aware that I had a lot of chatter in my head, so much that I needed to stop. I was working to heal my body, but my brain was driving me crazy. In my reading, there were many references to meditation to quiet the "monkey mind." I thought I should give it a try.

I followed all the directions to prepare myself for my first meditation session. I sewed a cushion that would be comfortable for me to sit on cross-legged. I found a place in my house to make a sacred alter and place important items, such as Tibetan bells, incense, and an incense holder. I was ready—but for what I really didn't know.

The first time I sat on my cushion, set a timer for ten minutes, and closed my eyes, I thought my head would explode with thoughts. *What am I doing? What do I need to be doing? Who do I need to call? Did I make all the doctor appointments? What is going on at work? Do they even know I am missing? Can they get along without me? And on and on and on. I heard the thoughts I had very loudly because there were no other distractions to drown out the constant chatter.* I didn't think my first meditation session went very well at all.

The next day, I followed the exact routine. I don't know why it didn't occur to me that I could try to meditate again the same day. Somehow, I thought I knew what to do and meditation was a once-a-day thing. This session didn't go any better. I had the same thoughts as the day before and a couple of new zingers: *"I didn't really know how to meditate"* and *"This is stupid."* The timer went off and I feared this meditation practice or my learning of it was not going to get better with this on-the-job-training approach.

I decided I needed to get more books about meditation. At the bookstore I headed straight to the Religion and Spirituality section. After leafing through many books, I found two new books that I wanted to read, *Synchrodestiny: The Spontaneous Fulfillment of Desire* by Deepak Chopra and *Autobiography of a Yogi* by Paramahansa Yogananda. Dr. Deepak Chopra is world famous for his gentle yet pervasive teachings, in addition to being a medical doctor. The Indian-born author and speaker is probably the foremost figure today in helping people find inner peace, health, and their spirituality through a variety of methods. A few of his famous quotes resonated with me:

- "In the midst of movement and chaos, keep stillness inside of you."
- "The less you open your heart to others, the more your heart suffers."
- "The way you think, the way you behave, the way you eat, can influence your life by 30 to 50 years."

He seemed to be addressing me. And he had arrived—or I had found him—in the nick of time. These new ideas that I was more than my identity, more than my thoughts, and my role in society were calling out to me. Given my choices—immobilizing illness and a return to a toxic business world—I bought a mat and the books on meditation.

The Chopra book looked like it would help me make sense of the tree experience and to see other things that I could only grasp once in a while. The Yogi book seemed like it would be a good way for me to learn more about meditation and maybe even yoga. And as I was reading Deepak Chopra's book, I realized that The Chopra Center was only fifteen miles from my house, at the Omni La Costa Resort and Spa in Carlsbad. I wondered what else I could learn there. So off I went.

When I arrived, I looked around the palm tree-ringed grounds, noting the delicately splashing fountain and vibrant flower beds. I experienced an instantaneous sense of peace. Not one that I would normally have. On the grass lawns, attractive, limber people sat in cross-legged yoga poses, as still as statues, yet relaxed. From somewhere, I heard faint celestial music. The center itself was a collection of white stucco buildings. The interiors continued the beatific style of the outdoors—natural motifs of the gardens—flooded with light and home to many lush plants and well-placed bookshelves. I inhaled the music with the aromas of the flower petals and light incense, carrying a breeze of peace. I was flooded with a sense of well-being that I had never known before.

Then, after contemplating several programs described in a brochure, I registered for the Primordial Sound Meditation course. As a novice meditator of two weeks, I knew I was doing it all wrong. This course seemed like a way to help me learn meditation. A week later, I began a new exploration, one that took me further into the invisible world that called to me, and with such a force that I was unable to turn away. After a brief introduction to the persons sitting on either side of me, I relaxed into my wide-eyed expectation for what was to come next in learning about Primordial Sound Meditation. I didn't even quite know what "primordial" meant. It seemed prehistoric to me.

In the workbook, I read the introduction from Deepak and one sentence struck me: "Meditation takes us beyond the confines of doubt, fear, and judgment of the mind, to the silence of our soul, our Spirit."

Isn't that what I was seeking?

My biggest take-away from Day One training was that I am not my thoughts. It was such a relief, because my thoughts were all over the place, and they were frequently negative during this time. *Why can't you figure all this out and get back to work? Are you just lazy? When are you going to get it together? If you were working harder or being smarter about this whole elevator thing, you would have figured it out and already been back to work. But instead, you are sitting in a meditation class. Really?*

The next question: *If I am not my thoughts, nor my identity that was firmly in place as a busy and successful executive, who was I then?*

The young female instructor, who was amazingly peaceful and soft in her demeanor, said that the thinker of my thoughts was my soul. *Whoa, whoa, whoa! I am the one thinking my thoughts. Who else would be doing the thinking here? My soul as separate from my thoughts?* It didn't make sense to me—yet.

The instructor then began to share about the integration of the physical body with the emotions and intellect in the subtle body and the spiritual body. She even said that meditation was an opportunity to integrate the bodies. I saw that I spent most of my time in the intellectual and emotional body and ignored the physical body. The spiritual body did not really even exist for me.

Perhaps this is what drove me to my current condition. So, what now?

Here is what she said: "At the most basic level, everything in the universe is sound or vibration. Then using ancient Vedic mathematics, the sound of the universe that corresponded with the time and place of birth was identified. This was the sound that predominated when we emerged through the gap into manifest creation. When this sound is incorporated into our mantra, it has the effect of drawing our attention inwards to reconnect it with the unbounded field of pure awareness, the Spirit."

I was baffled, and I wanted to know more.

Through a very sacred one-on-one meeting with the instructor, I was given my personal mantra for meditation. According to Deepak Chopra and the co-creator of Primoridial Sound Meditation, Dr. David Simon, who is now deceased, "A mantra is a specific sound or vibration—which when repeated silently—helps you to enter deeper levels of awareness. A Sanskrit term that translates as 'vehicle of the mind,' a mantra truly is a vehicle that takes you into quieter, more peaceful levels of the mind."

I wanted that connection.

Armed with the knowledge that meditation was perfect no matter what occurred, such as a gamut of wild ideas, I dived into my practice for thirty minutes each morning. I learned that when I had a lot of thoughts, I was just releasing a lot of stress and that my mantra gently brought me back to connection. On occasion, if I fell asleep, it was because I was tired. This idea of letting things just be as they are or as they unfold, was a new concept. Allowing what occurs to be okay, just as it is, and without judgment, was a relief.

A few times, I slipped into the gap of not thinking and not sleeping, and yet time passed. Those were the times that I was connected to eternity or Spirit. I didn't know what to make of it, but I was quite delighted that there were those times. I later discovered that meditation allowed me to own my day before it owned me.

As I continued attending my Primordial Sound Meditation class and kept practicing each morning, a new sense of calm pulsed through my being. I still did not know what was in store for me, but the future seemed to matter less than it had the previous month—or perhaps in my entire life. When I judged my situation, I noticed that I felt anxious and stressed.

Another paragraph from my workbook began to make a lot more sense. "In the West, we have been trained to put effort into everything we do. Meditation is the opposite, the less we do, the greater the rewards."

Now that was a new concept for me!

Dear Reader,

Principle #4 refers to "Activate Your Learning Gene." Explore ideas outside your wheelhouse. According to Deepak Chopra, MD, research shows that "We have an estimated 60,000-80,000 and unfortunately, many of the same thoughts we had yesterday, last week, and last year." The way to get around these thoughts is meditation, which according to Chopra, is a powerful practice for going beyond habitual, conditioned thought patterns into a state of expanded awareness.

- *What thoughts repeatedly float through your mind, creating distraction and anxiety?*
- *What new concepts or beliefs are calling for your attention?*
- *What do you do to tame the monkey mind?*

CHAPTER 9

MY CLAIM TO FAME

As I continued to meditate daily, I began to contemplate what would it be like to not work in the world of corporate. I had been working since I was fourteen years old and now at forty-five, I was a bit tired of it. I thought back to some thoughts that I had the previous year of feeling like I was caught in a spider web—one of those nylon, bungee webs that were used to hold down cargo in the back of a pick-up truck. It was a space of wishing I was someplace else—without knowing where, just any place different than where I was.

Dana and I were walking one evening that previous year and I said, "Why don't we just quit working, sell all our possessions, and travel?" Hearing myself say those words filled me with a sense of relief.

She simply said, "Do you have a plan of what we would do after this shedding activity?"

"I hadn't thought that far yet. But it would be an adventure, and we'll just figure it out," I replied.

She said in her perfectly calm Dana-way, "Let's talk about it more when you have a plan."

One year later, I was circling around to the same place only now I was on disability leave and starting to realize that maybe work was making me sick.

I literally felt like I was going to die if I went back to work. I could not imagine going back to getting up at 6:00 a.m., getting to work by 7:00 a.m., and working until 6:00 or 7:00 p.m., only to do it all over again the next day. I imagined that I would once again attend meetings that seemed to not matter, and implement projects that did not positively impact the world or make a bit of difference to anyone, except the corporation that was paying my salary and needed it done to be paid by the client.

It all seemed so empty and devoid of purpose. The entire arrangement of economics and capitalism suddenly seemed wrong to me. I was not seeing the big picture, nor seeing the good that is present in economics and capitalism. At that point, I could no longer see any redeeming value to return to work. And, yet, I was having to consider my next step, as my time on the disability roll was coming to an end.

The cardiologist thought my heart valve needed to be replaced as it was not closing properly and there was blood leakage back into the ventricle. My neurologist and endocrinologist could not find an issue to treat with medication or surgery. Since all my vital signs were improving, and I had refused the heart valve diagnosis and surgery, I would soon be released from medical leave and pronounced fit for work. Four months ago, my sole purpose was to figure out my health challenge, resolve it, and get back to work. Now, I wanted nothing to do with returning to that position or any job for that matter. The only clarity I had was that I needed to do something else, because my very existence depended on it. I could not and would not sacrifice myself to help a corporation earn a buck.

With that great clarity, I was in the space of the unknown. I had to try something new. I remembered the Albert Einstein quote, "No problem can be solved from the same level of consciousness that created it."

I was totally lost.

Earlier in my life, I strongly identified with the hard-working, barely scraping by, paycheck-to-paycheck people who were my dear friends and co-workers in my first and second factory jobs. In the 1970s, there were many jobs for unskilled laborers who were willing to listen to instructions and do manual and repetitive tasks in a factory—such was my work life through my high school years. In order to earn enough money to get out on my own, I worked odd jobs, summers, and then evenings while I was finishing high school.

Having proven myself with the piecework at fourteen years old, Zig and Ruth gave me a job every summer, as well as weekends and evenings to work in their electronics factory. While still in high school, I worked 4:00-8:00 p.m. Monday through Friday and all-day Saturdays to earn money for my "escape from home" savings account.

The factory crew would get off work at 3:30 p.m. and they would leave me notes on what jobs needed to be completed that night in preparation for the work crew that came back in at 6:30 a.m. the next morning. Usually, this job was to run the wave solder machine so the circuit boards would be ready for the ladies to clean up the solder bridges and replace circuit pads. Then the circuit cards would be ready to test and ship the next day. Wave soldering was pretty messy, and I doubt that the current EPA and OSHA laws would have allowed me to breathe the toxic fumes from the mix of solvents that I was accustomed to smelling. I didn't really care. I just knew I was good at my job, my bank account was growing, and that I was continually challenged with learning all the tasks in the factory because I was the night shift.

Zig asked me one day if I liked being the troubleshooter of the factory. I had to ask him what the word meant because I had never heard the word before.

"Kind of like a utility player. Somebody that can roam around the factory and do any job, but is not saddled with one job," he patiently explained.

"Yes, I like being the troubleshooter, because I like variety and the challenge to learn new things," I said, as I was working on building oxygen monitor stands for the sixth day in a row.

He said, "How many of those stands can you build in a day?"

Not knowing why he asked, I proudly said, "200!" This was actually the most I had built in one day of busting my butt. My normal rate was to make about 180 a day.

Coming purely from a place of trying to motivate and reward me, he kindly said, "I will pay you an extra dime for every stand over 200 that you build in a day!"

Inside, I sank. *Why didn't I say 180? I could have immediately made an extra $2 a day.*

I took it as a personal challenge and built 217 the next day. I made 213 the following day and by the third day I was at 210. I was quickly losing ground. I was so happy the job was done by the end of that week, as I had earned an additional $7 on my paycheck.

What I didn't know was that by creating a nearly impossible goal, I had learned to eliminate any unnecessary movement by setting up all my materials in a perfect and useful order and creating a human assembly line. Fifteen years later, efficiency in business would be my claim to fame while working with the team to save my company tens of millions by eliminating $1.5M dollars of cost per aircraft housing.

Dear Reader,

It's important to acknowledge what we're good at and at the same time realize that any strengths when overused can become weaknesses. This can be particularly dangerous if we are stuck in situations that might not be the best for our health and well-being.

- *What is your claim to fame?*
- *How do you benefit from it?*
- *Where might your skills be applicable to a new environment?*

CHAPTER 10

PUSHING THROUGH RESISTANCE

───────────────

IN MY SECOND FACTORY JOB, I worked in a transformer factory for six years and enjoyed nearly every minute of it. I printed the company name, part number, and manufacturing date on transformers. Because printing was the last production function prior to shipping the customer's order out the door, I was able to learn many of the production jobs in the factory because I didn't have a lot of work early in the week. Most of my printing work was on Thursday and Friday mornings. Then on Friday afternoons, I would move to the shipping area to pack and ship the order to make our sales numbers that week.

After accumulating an understanding of many of the jobs and starting to create estimates about how long jobs took in each function, I thought it would be useful to create a factory work flow schedule. I had a natural talent for seeing the bottlenecks and figuring out how to even the production flow. I imagined that smoothing out the workflow would move more work through the factory, and we would produce more sales. They never told me that I couldn't do it, so I wrote out factory schedules to make the work flow easier. It also entailed moving resources to release the bottlenecks. Danny Becerra, my supervisor and lifelong cheerleader and friend, welcomed the help as he spent a good portion of his time working on the personnel issues with a factory of fifty people.

During a factory visit by the president of the parent company, I was called into the general manager's office. The office had a plate glass window from which to view the factory. There was no hiding from my co-workers that I had been summoned to the office and that the general manager and the president were talking to me. I asked Danny to join me, because I was scared and thought that I was about to lose my job. He told me to go without him, and because they were kind, it would all be fine for me. So, I walked into the office with rounded shoulders and was leery of making eye contact. After being introduced to the president, Mr. Walton, and shaking his hand, he got right down to business.

"Why haven't you gone to college? You are too smart to be on a factory floor for the rest of your life," he said. There was a compassionate tone to his voice that I wasn't accustomed to, and it reflected in his brown eyes.

I was stunned and didn't know what to say. Thank you was the first thing that I thought to say. As I regained my composure, I realized that I needed my best possible reason for this man.

"I like working and don't want to go to college. I worked all through high school and had tried a semester of community college at night school and found that I was too tired working and going to school at the same time. So, I just want to work," I shared with my best twenty-year old logic.

"You will never earn much more than you make today without a college education," he explained.

"I make $20,500 a year and that is more than I have ever made in my life. I am very happy with my salary level and my work because I have time to do other things that I enjoy doing in my life," I said.

I proceeded to tell him that I played on the company co-ed softball team and volunteered at the company walk-a-thons, thinking that he would be impressed with my additional company activities beyond my job. I realized later that I was missing the whole point. He really didn't care what I did for the company on or off the job; he wanted me to get an education.

He was exasperated with me and said, "I want you to research the colleges in town, and in thirty days, I want a report on the college you could attend."

Worried about questioning authority, I said "ok" and left the office. *Great! Now I have somebody on my butt to go to school. The last years had been so much fun with not going to school.*

Heading back to my office, I concocted a story about what I would tell everyone else in the factory about my meeting with the president. I decided it would simply be that he was asking about the production levels that we could obtain. That would satisfy everyone that asked.

Danny stopped me before I was able to speak to anyone else. "What happened in there?"

Looking into his caring brown eyes made me want to cry. "They want me to go to college."

"Good for you! You really need to do this, Cindy." He put his arm around me in a fatherly way. "You're too smart to let this go. People don't just hand people opportunities," he said, softly. "It's a gift."

He was right, although I struggled with being seen and acknowledged for my work. Safety came by flying under the radar. In truth, I really didn't know that what I did was special. I did what came naturally to me. And I knew I needed to honor this man who invited me into his family and treated me like one of his daughters. Danny was the antithesis of my father—soft-spoken, dapper, and kind. He showed me what a safe loving family could be like. With that in mind, I moved forward with the president's request, even if I wasn't completely convinced that it was the right move for me.

I wrote out the questions I would ask the three colleges in town. I was most interested in teaching so decided that I would ask about how long it would take and how much money it would cost to get a teaching credential. After speaking with staff at San Diego State University (SDSU), University of California at San Diego (UCSD), and University of San Diego (USD), I discovered that it would take me at least eight years of night school and about $1,500 to get my teaching credential.

These answers seemed absolutely ridiculous to me. So, I asked a teacher friend of mine about getting a degree. She said it was five years of day school, so eight years of night school was probably right. She then showed me the salary scale for teachers. It was like a spreadsheet with the x-axis showing the years of service and the y-axis showing the degrees and certifications earned. When I followed my finger along the bachelor's degree and the first year of service, I realized that my entry-level salary after eight years of schooling would be $20,500. The exact same amount that I was earning now! I just didn't see the point in going back to school.

After completing my research for the three universities and writing down the time and costs, I met with Mr. Walton and explained to him that the data clearly showed that it would take too long and cost too much money to earn a degree. I made a very strong point about the $20,500 starting salary after eight years and figured he would just drop the whole thing. It seemed so obvious to me that it was a dumb idea. To his credit, he was relentless.

"I won't take no for an answer" he said. "I want you to take another thirty days and research getting a business degree. You clearly have a business mind," he said. "I have heard about and seen the systems and methods you have created that make the factory work better, and I don't want your natural talent to go to waste."

"And add National University to your list for research. It is a new university that just opened and caters to working adults, like you," he rose from behind the desk and shook my hand, indicating that our meeting was now over.

His remark about me being an adult seized my attention. This was the first time somebody had referred to me as an adult, even though I had taken that role on years before. I still wasn't thrilled about going to school, and I really didn't know what business was about. I just knew that I knew how to work in factories.

Once again, I called the three universities, and this time I asked about getting a bachelor's degree in business. Each of the schools' business degrees were about the same cost as the teaching degree that I had previously inquired about but about one and half years less in duration than the teaching degree. That was promising, but six years of night school was not.

Then, I called National University and discovered that they taught a course a month. Classes met two nights a week and every other Saturday. The entire undergraduate degree would take me forty-eight months. The admissions person told me I could take tests to get up to ten courses waived. If I passed those tests along with my one semester of three courses that would transfer from the community college, I could finish in about three years. The catch was that it was expensive. It would cost about $6,000 for the entire degree.

I assembled all my information for my next meeting with Mr. Walton. I was still not enthused to go to school, but if I had to choose one, I was going for the least amount of time as possible. I walked confidently into the meeting with copies of my handwritten analysis and explained my analysis to Mr. Walton and the general manager.

Mr. Walton nodded and I knew he was impressed with my analysis. "The company will pay for 66% of your tuition. You need to pay for 33% and your books. Which one will you attend?"

"I am not interested in attending school," I replied.

"I want you to attend one semester and then report back." He stared at me and waited for my response.

Brother, this guy was not going to give up. Would my job be on the line, if I didn't go to school? I had to tell him something. I calmly said, "I will go to National University and take three courses and then report back to you." I walked out of the office and went back to work, fretting about going back to school.

Why would I add stress back to my life and go to night school while working full time? It doesn't make any sense to me.

I completed my admissions paperwork for National University and registered for three classes as an undergrad with a business major. My first class was in April, and with any amount of luck, I planned to be finished with this little experiment by the end of June—just in time for a wonderful sun-filled summer in San Diego. My first class was public speaking, my second was business math, and the third was psychology. I aced the courses, and by the middle of the second class, I was hooked on school again. When I reported back to Mr. Walton in July, I had applied and was approved for a $2,000 student loan, passed seven of ten tests on the College Level Entry Program (CLEP), had declared a Business major with an emphasis in Management Information System (MIS), and registered for my remaining courses.

This time, I walked into our meeting with a little swagger because I was on a path of learning that I sensed would be good for me. It even seemed like it might be fun. Mr. Walton had a knowing look on his face and congratulated me on my decision to go back to school.

"Grace is not knowledge or reason but the amount of light in our souls," says Pope Francis. I'm convinced that Mr. Walton saw the light in my soul—a light I just didn't see until much later in my life.

After completing my undergrad degree, I decided I was on a studying roll and went on to get my graduate degree, a Master's in Business Administration (MBA) with an emphasis in Information Technology (IT). It was this degree that opened all the doors to managing information technology projects for the next twenty years.

Looking back, I can detect my own self-sabotaging pattern showing its ugly head in my resistance to advancement, my own negative reasoning. Luckily, my self-preservation instinct kicked in, and I grabbed the opportunity to prevail and excel.

Dear Reader,

Principle #5 refers to "See Your Colleagues Bigger than They See Themselves." Mr. Walton saw me bigger than I could see myself. He pulled and pushed me into something that I didn't know. At the time, I didn't want the attention; however, it was one of the best things that ever happened to me.

- *When has someone seen you bigger than you see yourself?*
- *When have you seen someone bigger than they see themselves?*
- *What did you do to bring them into this reality?*

CHAPTER 11

DISCOVERING A NEW WAY

MY MEDITATIONS WERE so deep and restorative. I wanted to just be in that place for twenty-four hours a day. Yet, I didn't see how I could stay in this contemplative space all the time and live a productive and successful life. It seemed as though I could either be a driven and successful executive with a very clear understanding of an endgame, or I could be in this contemplative, relaxed, and blissful place. They seemed opposite to me. I began to contemplate what a new way could be. I did not yet understand the Buddhist concept of a middle way, simply described as a rejection of extremes, a path of moderation. And neither of these current options seemed doable.

So, what was I to do? I could find a different job, but what would it be? How would that be any different than what I have done? And in thirty days would be doing again, if I didn't get it together and find my new thing.

The one thing I did know was that I had to take care of my own financial well-being. I needed to financially contribute to our household and our relationship. Yet, every thought I had, provided a very clear and rational reason why I could not return to corporate. When I went through the pros and cons about all possibilities, not one idea came through as something that was remotely possible or doable. More importantly, nothing seemed that interesting. I had yet to learn that joy and bliss come from aligning with my soul's true calling. Heck, I had just barely learned that I had a soul, and that I was not my feelings or my thoughts. It all seemed so alien to me.

Carefully and sacredly, each day, I would light incense and a candle, set my timer, and comfortably sit in my chair (I had already abandoned my floor cushion) with my bare feet planted firmly on the floor and my spine erect to connect to my newfound soul. The aroma of incense would shroud me with a mantle of well-being. Concentrating on the candle's flame and hearing the candlewick sputtering gave me comfort as I silently repeated my primordial chant in the privacy of my own mind as I slipped away.

When the Tibetan bell timer rang, I slowly and gently brought my hands together in front of my heart in a prayer pose and said aloud, "Namaste," the sound of which vibrated through my being—and which meant that I was beginning to honor the divinity within my own being.

The place I traveled to for those thirty minutes wasn't like sleep, nor was I dreaming. The best my rational mind could do was to describe it like a crack in this dimension that I was squeezing through each day. My connection with this new place was so seductive that I could not imagine not meditating. And I also hoped that maybe, just maybe, through my meditation practice, guidance would reveal itself on what I was to do in my life. I finally gave up on the idea that my reasoning mind could solve this! Yet, I kept reading for more clues and inspiration, particularly from Chopra's *Synchrodestiny*. It, however, did not keep me from worry. So, I continued my search. Rationally, I knew there was nothing to save me from my inevitable return to work. The time would come when my disability would be over and I would be given a clean bill of health. My body was doing well, but the rest of me was now in a new turmoil. *What am I doing? Where am I going?* I didn't know those answers. What I did know was that I would not be staying at CSC for long—only long enough to find my new chapter and new adventure. That was somehow comforting to me.

When I returned to work, all my colleagues were warm and fun and welcomed me back with open arms. The project had moved along and was in the last stages of completion. Re-inserting me into the project made no sense to the client, the business, or even to me. Instead, as a valued employee, I was placed into another position where I could contribute and manage large IT accounts. I was grateful to my colleagues for the job and inwardly was equally clear this was temporary. I knew I would do my best work. However, I was going to create and live by new boundaries. The first was that I would not work the insane hours I had worked prior to my elevator incident. I eased back into a more usual routine of working forty hours as opposed to my previous grueling schedule of seventy hours per week, which gave me plenty of time to meditate in the morning, read at night, and continue my exploration into what I wanted to do in the future.

Since I had attended classes at the Chopra Center, I received a newsletter in the mail about a conference in Puerto Rico called "An Alliance for New Humanity" with global dignitaries and thought leaders on the conference agenda. Deepak Chopra was speaking and the Master of Ceremonies. Al Gore, former Vice President of the United States and now a leading spokesperson on the environment, was also speaking. Oscar Arias, the former President of Costa Rica and Nobel Peace Prize recipient for his role in the Central American peace accords in Nicaragua, was another headliner. As Dana and I had vacationed in Costa Rica a few years earlier, Costa Rican President Arias and the name Costa Rica itself caught my fleeting eye. President Arias was also described as one of the founding members of the United Nations University for Peace.

Their mission statement was alluring: *"to provide humanity with an international institution of higher education for peace with the aim of promoting among all human beings the spirit of understanding, tolerance and peaceful coexistence, to stimulate cooperation among peoples and to help lessen obstacles and threats to world peace and progress, in keeping with the noble aspirations proclaimed in the Charter of the United Nations."*

The conference topics and speakers caught my attention, but I had just returned to work, and I didn't really have the money to attend. I threw the newsletter in the trash. A couple of days later, I was reading *Spirituality and Health* magazine, and there was an advertisement and brief article on yoga retreats in Costa Rica. There was a beautiful picture of the rain forest and a description of the amazing wildlife viewing for intrepid travelers.

I was reminded of our Costa Rican vacation when Dana and I had soaked in those natural hot springs in the shadow of the volcano, Arenal. We had zip-lined across the cloud forests in Monteverde. And we had ventured out to the remote Oso Peninsula to hike in the first growth rain forests. It was so remote that we had flown from San Jose (capital of Costa Rica) in a prop plane that landed in a banana field. This was next to the mysterious granite spheres. After exploring the field with various sized spheres, we were then picked up by a jitney bus and whisked through palm groves to a beyond Disneyland-like jungle cruise boat, where we navigated through a narrow river with crocodiles until it opened into the blue-blue Pacific Ocean. Then, the boat turned into a speedboat racing south and parallel to the land. After about twenty minutes, we slowed and pulled into an inlet where tractors awaited our arrival. We waded ashore and climbed onto the tractor for the haul up the hill to the cabanas on the edge of the rain forest and our home for the next four days. I remembered that experience with great fondness, as I turned the pages to the next article.

One evening, when Dana was at a public meeting, I decided to crawl into bed early and read *Autobiography of a Yogi,* by Paramahansa Yogananda, who was born in India in 1893. He shares his spiritual journey, quest for truth, and reveals the underlying unity of the great religions of East and West. Additionally, the book is also a comprehensive introduction to the whole science and philosophy of yoga. I was rapt with attention to the stories about his solitary and contemplative practices. Parallels or at least similarities were obvious between my experiences and his. I could not wait to go to bed each night to discover and enjoy his next adventures. It had moved to the top of my book pile, and this was my new go-to book on the nightstand. I had just finished the section where he was studying with his master, and he had an experience of Cosmic Consciousness. Upon returning into his present body state, his master explained, "Those who attain Self-realization on earth live a two-fold experience. Consciously performing their work in the world, while they are also immersed in an inward beatitude."

Both states could co-exist. But how?

I was drifting off to sleep as these thoughts swirled through my mind. As I placed the book on my nightstand, I saw the back cover, for the first time. There was an endorsement from Dr. Robert Muller, Former United Nations Assistant Secretary-General and Chancellor, UN University for Peace, Costa Rica. I bolted up in bed in a hyper-alert state.

What am I being guided to do here? I couldn't hear about Costa Rica three times in less than a month and believe it is coincidental.

Dr. Chopra explains in *Synchrodestiny* that there are no coincidences—just guidance. I immediately went to my computer and Googled United Nations University for Peace in Costa Rica. There it was. A unique university, established by the UN in 1980. A small quaint building set on a spectacular 781-acre campus donated by the Costa Rican government, high in the mountains west of San Jose, Costa Rica, amidst coffee plantations and one of the largest pristine rain forests in the world.

The university appeared as an egalitarian Eden, a sanctuary for rational thinking and preparation to save the world. It offered courses in five fields of study: International Law, Environmental Studies, International Peace and Conflict Studies, Gender Topics, and Peace Education. As I perused the website, I was wondering if this was a possibility for me. Questions flooded into my consciousness.

Is this a distance learning degree? No, it is residential. Okay that is a problem, I thought. Is there a PhD series? No, only master's programs. Well, I already have a master's degree. Seems weird. Probably two years of study? No, just one year. It must be taught in Spanish? No, it is in English. Hmm. It must be cost prohibitive? No, just $18,000 per year. Costly to live there? No, estimated at $700-$800 per month.

I noticed myself sweating, and as I looked for reasons why this was not mine to do—I found very few. Printing out the coursework for three of the degrees, I grabbed my highlighter and crawled back into bed.

I read the coursework with interest and awe. Mostly, I didn't understand how or why anyone would want a liberal arts degree, areas I knew absolutely nothing about. I could not quite let myself imagine my answer being "yes," but I was intrigued.

Just then, I heard the garage door and Dana arrive home. I had learned early in our relationship not to bring up important items late at night. I tended to be the type that blurted out my ideas and then got irritated and criticized her if she was too tired to listen or engage. She was walking down the hall as I contemplated what to do with the printouts.

"How was your night meeting?" I casually asked, like our world was not about to be turned upside down, as I placed the papers on the nightstand.

"Oh, it was fine. You know the usual. Discussions and debates that take way too long to finally make the decision that was obvious in the first ten minutes," she said in her calm Dana-way. As she climbed into bed, she asked, "What are you reading?"

I said, "*The Autobiography of a Yogi*. You remember; I told you about it a while ago."

She pointed and said, "No, I mean the highlighted printouts."

"Nothing really," I said trying to be casual and keeping the anxiousness out of my voice.

"Let me see them," she asked.

I held my breath as I handed her the pile of stapled and highlighted papers.

She breezily flipped through them in her smart executive way and re-organized the papers. She handed them back to me with a clipped, "I think this is the one you should do."

I could not breathe. I was just plain freaked out! My "final" obstacle had been removed.

Dear Reader,

Logic can often be our biggest nemesis. We frequently make arguments as to why something won't work or isn't a good fit for us. Used judiciously and consciously, logic is a great skill set. When we use our logic to make an argument against something that is calling us to a higher level of consciousness or opportunity, we perpetuate the old story and we remain stuck in our current, often unhealthy circumstances.

- *What synchronicities are calling your attention?*
- *What are they asking of you?*
- *How are you responding?*

CHAPTER 12

FEAR OF CHANGE

A<small>T ABOUT</small> 5:00 A.M. I finally got up from bed and made coffee and sat in the living room. The idea of letting go of a life I had worked so hard for in favor of a blissed out, peace-and-love life seemed weird. The bliss I experienced internally through meditation was okay, but I had no idea what actually being that person looked like externally. I didn't want to be judged by others as a freak. I had worked hard to build a very successful life and career. It seemed wrong to just let that go. I was in a quandary of epic proportions. As I sat bleary-eyed with my coffee and my anxious monkey mind, I contemplated—no—I worried about this new idea that was freaking me out to my very core.

At seven, Dana got up and made some coffee and we sat in silence. She is very good at reading my moods and treading lightly when she feels that is what I need. "Let's have coffee in the Jacuzzi this morning," she offered, eyeing me warily.

"That will really feel good. I didn't sleep at all last night," I casually mentioned.

She didn't comment, as we got into the Jacuzzi on this Friday morning in early January 2004. San Diego is very comfortable in January and while it was a little brisk, 60 degrees, the 102-degree water felt very soothing to my very scared being. We watched the hummingbirds enjoying the nectar of the brightly colored flowers in our back yard. House finches, sparrows, and Dana's favorite bird, the cedar wax wings, came to the water fountain to bathe and enjoy the morning sunshine with no awareness of the two of us sitting in the Jacuzzi. Slowly, I felt the tension in my body melt away.

Thirty minutes later, I was chopping zucchini, tomatoes, and onions for the veggie scramble when Dana sensed I'd be open to discussion. "What are you afraid of?"

The question startled me so that I almost sliced my finger, right along with the vegetables. I put the knife down and turned to her. "Everything! Where do I start? I am afraid to quit my job. I am afraid of not making money. I am afraid of moving to Costa Rica and leaving you here. What if our relationship is not strong enough for that? I am afraid I won't know how to study anymore since it has been twenty years since my MBA. I am afraid to live in another country. I am afraid of getting sick again. I am afraid of giving up my career path and my plan to retire at fifty-five with a healthy 401k. I am afraid of just running away," I blurted out with all the courage I could muster. On the edge of tears, I resumed cutting my vegetables.

"Seems like a lot of self-judgment," she said, as she set the table for breakfast. "You might want to consider that you have been asking for guidance in your meditations and now that you have been given clear guidance, you are ignoring it."

"I am sure you are right." Now the tears were streaming. "It's just hard to trust that it's the right thing to do!"

We went about our Friday, doing house and yard chores and running errands. The back yard was a veritable paradise—a well-manicured lawn and beautiful gardens with flowers and plants that required much love and attention to maintain their beauty. This was Dana's palette. She enjoyed grounding herself in the soil of Mother Earth and watching the plants, bushes, and trees grow into lush expressions of their natural beauty. She loved going to the nursery and picking out different plants for specific locations in the yard that would grow into the rich picture that was ever-evolving in her mind's eye. While I didn't want to be a gardener or a farmer, I was envious of her natural attraction and talent for being with the plant life. After a day in the yard, she was tired, but exhilarated by the experience.

We didn't talk about that wild Costa Rica idea again until Saturday. However, it was never far from my mind. Every time I thought of going to the United Nations University for Peace in Costa Rica, my pulse quickened, my heart pounded, and my palms sweat. Any attempts at meditation were useless. I was steeped in pure unadulterated fear. I had not felt this fearful since I was a child.

By Saturday, I had ruminated about it long enough and decided I was ready to talk again. "Can we take some time to discuss the concerns I have about Costa Rica?"

"I look forward to it," Dana said. "Anytime you are ready, I am here and willing to listen."

It was not by accident that Dana and I became life partners. We met the first time in the 1970s. She and my first partner went to undergraduate school together at San Diego State University. I thought she was extremely smart, knowledgeable, interesting, fun, and she had an innate curiosity about other people and life. Over the next many years, Dana and I would run into each other at various parties or events and would quickly catch up on our lives and part ways until the next time our paths crossed. We didn't run in the same circles, but sure enjoyed seeing one another when we would have chance meetings over the next two plus decades.

Her curiosity for learning and knowing more about life is how we reconnected through a mutual friend in 1999. Dana had attended a workshop and had asked a mutual friend how she could keep the new thoughts and paradigms alive in her life. Our mutual friend suggested she phone me and talk about it as I had also attended the workshop several years earlier.

It was from this place of intellectual curiosity and genuine interest in me and my life journey that Dana was able to listen to me without judgment and self-interest—although as my life partner, my decisions would surely have an impact on her.

Dana said, "Let's take the concerns one at a time and see if we can understand more about them." This seemed like the right approach because I was actually getting tired of having the same thoughts over and over in my mind to only wind up at the same fearful spot.

We started on the easier items, "Tell me about your concerns in knowing how to study at forty-five years old."

I started with, "I am afraid that I won't be able to keep up with the twenty-somethings that will be getting their graduate degree."

"You have always been a good student, and during your career you have continued to learn new things at a remarkable pace," she responded. "As a lifelong learner, you won't be able to *not* do a good job studying and keeping up with the twenty-somethings. You will be surprised because they will learn a lot from you."

Well, that is an interesting perspective. "You are probably right. I guess that is not really an issue after all. The concerns are going to get harder now," I said as we both laughed.

"Let's talk about the cost of this master's program," Dana said. "It is $18,000, and we have enough money in the bank to just write a check for that. What is the concern?"

I felt a pang in my stomach and declared, "That doesn't feel right. I don't want you or our joint account to pay for my degree. I want to pay for it myself."

"Then, how about you take $18,000 from the cash value of your life insurance policy?"

I was beginning to see this wasn't as difficult as I was making it out to be.

"What about the living expenses for Costa Rica?" she asked.

"I will need another $6-8,000 for the year." I'd already played with the numbers in my head multiple times. "And I have enough in my policy for that as well. Hypothetically, of course," I said with a grin. I was noticing a spot inside of me that was warming to this plan.

She smiled and then prodded a little deeper. "What about stepping off the career ladder, retirement at fifty-five, and the 401k?"

That question triggered a reaction so deep and intense that I cried so hard that I could not catch my breath. Snot was running from my nose and the tears stung my eyes as they rolled down my face. I was gulping as I tried to catch my breath. Dana held me while I cried. When I was finally all cried out, I had a massive headache. We took a little breather.

It was a new experience for me to be with raw and incomplete emotions. I had always been very direct and did not let issues linger. When issues arose, I was the first to say, "Let's talk about it." I know there is a solution here and dialogue is the bridge to the other side.

Yet, in this instance, I was at a loss. I was once again in the abyss of not knowing.

Sunday morning, we went to The Center for Spiritual Living for our spiritual nourishment, and I enjoyed the distraction from talking about Costa Rica. During the services, I asked my inner Spirit for strength, courage, and clarity as I explored whether or not Costa Rica was the next chapter in my life or not.

Refueled with energy and courage, Dana and I decided to talk again on Sunday afternoon. We picked up where we left off Saturday afternoon, when I had inexplicably gone into crying convulsions. "What is it about stepping off the career ladder, retirement at fifty-five, and the 401k that had such an emotional reaction?" Dana asked.

"There is something invisible here that I don't quite know about or understand," I explained. "Can you ask me more questions to help me figure it out?"

She said, "What does the career ladder, retirement, and the 401k represent to you?"

I just sat for a few moments and checked into the place in my heart, that I had learned through my meditation and reading the previous few months, that knows the truth. I shared, "It seems like it is not financial security because I know that I am capable of earning enough money to be financially secure. Of course, I will miss at least a year of earning a healthy income. It is a year that I won't get back, and I know that I am at my peak earning potential. It all seems rather crazy to think about quitting now. That is all I can discern, at this point."

She stated quietly, "That doesn't seem like it. You would not have had such an emotional reaction if that was it."

Once again, I closed my eyes and went to that place inside of me that knows. After a couple of minutes, I began to cry. I had found it. "Money, a steady income, and money in retirement represent safety to me," I said as it all became clear to me, through more tears.

At fourteen years old, I knew money was my ticket to safety and freedom. At seventeen years old, I left my childhood home and made my way on my own because of the money I earned. When I was able to speak again I said, "My physical and emotional safety were collapsed onto the concept of having enough money. Translated, if I didn't earn an income, I was not safe. That is what quitting work and stepping off the career ladder represented. I would not be safe."

Dana said with deep love and compassion, "We will put money in an account in Costa Rica that you can use anytime you want it or need it. How much money should we deposit for you to feel safe? $1,000, $5,000, $10,000, $25,000? How much?"

I said, "I think $5,000 would be enough."

Once again, I felt like all the negative associations with this idea to move to Costa Rica were disappearing. With Dana's help, I was conquering all the demons that were in my head about taking the next step in my life and quite possibly my career.

However, there was one last big concern: *Would our relationship endure the separation?* I felt bad about leaving her while I went on a life adventure figuring out a new career for myself. Yet, I was too emotionally spent to talk anymore. Instead, we went about enjoying the rest of our day, connecting at the deepest level with another human being, despite the vulnerabilities.

By that night, I was ready to bring the relationship topic back again. With Dana's red wine and my O'Doul's, we went back to the Jacuzzi for our next awesome discussion. There is really nothing better than talking with the one you love in a Jacuzzi with a nice drink in your hand. In that instant, everything felt possible! This time, I started the conversation, "How are we going to keep our relationship and passion alive when we live in two different countries?"

Dana started with, "Ever since we have been together, you have traveled for your job. We would do it the same way we always do it. We talk on the phone every day. We connect and talk about our day and share our love for each other. We would maintain our gratitude for this life and relationship we have created together. That's how!"

"Aren't you afraid?" I asked.

"Sure. But we can't live our life afraid. We are meant to live with joy and without fear. We can do this. Besides, I have a lot going on here with my family and their various illnesses and situations. The time will go by fast. You should not let this fear stop you from saying "yes." I would never tell you not to go. As a matter of fact, I am telling you that I think you should go. It will be good for you and that will be good for us."

I cried tears of joy and said, "I am so lucky that you are my life partner. Thank you. And, I am still not convinced that I am going to go to Costa Rica."

That night, as I read *The Autobiography of a Yogi,* I imagined what it would be like to live in another place in the world, having new, interesting experiences. I drifted off with a smile on my face and slept like a baby.

On Monday night, we decided that we would bring home take-out food and watch President Bush's 2004 State of the Union address. We settled on the couch with our food and drinks. We were in two wars and Americans were agitated and divided at that time, as they are right now.

As we listened, we were opposed to almost every policy that was described. As the speech continued, we were complaining and loudly talking back to the television. We did not believe there were weapons of mass destruction in Iraq and did not at all believe that war was the answer—to anything. The idea of retaliation for 9/11 was an eye-for-an-eye approach, and we believed more in Dr. Martin Luther King's statement that, "Man must evolve for all human conflict, a method which rejects revenge, aggression, and retaliation. The foundation of such a method is love."

I could feel myself leaving my very peaceful place just listening to the president. *I am not going to sit on this couch one more moment and complain about why I don't like American foreign policy or the president's decisions. I need to do something else, however small it might be! I had to take an action of my own!*

It was in that moment that I told Dana, "I am going to apply to the United Nations University for Peace for admittance to the master's degree in International Peace and Conflict Studies and Peace Education. If it is meant to be, I will be accepted. If it is not, my application will be declined."

There it was, the decision. All the discussions over the weekend had positioned me squarely on the edge of the cliff. The State of the Union pushed me over the edge. That decision would change my life forever. Much like the 18th century German poet Goethe so famously said:

"Until one is committed, there is hesitancy, the chance to draw back— Concerning all acts of initiative (and creation), there is one elementary truth that ignorance of which kills countless ideas and splendid plans: that the moment one definitely commits oneself, then Providence moves too. All sorts of things occur to help one that would never otherwise have occurred. A whole stream of events issues from the decision, raising in one's favor all manner of unforeseen incidents and meetings and material assistance, which no man could have dreamed would have come his way. Whatever you can do, or dream you can do, begin it. Boldness has genius, power, and magic in it. Begin it now."

- Johann Wolfgang von Goethe

I was committed.

Dear Reader,

Principle #6 refers to "Move to Action," without knowing all the steps. According to Dr. Deborah Sandella, in her book, Goodbye, Hurt & Pain, *fear creates "a biochemical reaction that expresses as fight, flight, freeze, or faint." Very often our fears prevent us from stepping out into a greater opportunity. Our past experiences are often the source of fear and are imbedded in the body. We may not even know that it's there and we often do not give voice to it or explore it because it's so invisible to us. It's part of the fabric to who we are. We need to face our fears and name them, and then say, "I'm still scared to death and I'm doing it anyway." I invite you to contemplate the following:*

- *What are some of your fears?*
- *What do you base your safety and freedom upon?*
- *What new path is requiring a commitment from you?*

Mom and Dad Dating, 1952

Mom and Cindy, 1958

Cindy, Deb, and Pam, 1964

Dad, Career Navy Man, 1972

Mom, Pam, Deb, and Cindy, 1972

Jungle View from Casita, 2004

Alphonse at UPEACE, 2004

African friends Alphonse, Patrick, Emmanual, Christine, 2004

Muzy at Weekend Party, 2005.

La Carpio Neighborhood, 2005.

La Carpio Elementary School, 2005

Tory on UPEACE Bus, 2004.

UPEACE Graduation Ceremony, 2005

Dana Smith

Mom, Cindy, and Dana at UPEACE Graduation, 2005.

UPEACE Graduation Celebration, 2005.

Dana, Cindy, and Woodstock 2013.

Cindy in Coaching Session, 2013.

Dana and Cindy at Mexico Ruins, 2015.

Client Passion and Purpose Session, 2016.

Danny and Delphi Becerra, 65th Wedding Anniversary 2016.

Cindy, Mom, and Deb, 2017.

Client Group, Strategic Planning, 2017.

Superhero Leadership Conference, 2017.

Florence, Dana, and Alphonse in Sweden, 2017.

Cindy and Muzy, Stockholm, 2017.

Team Planning Landscape Project, 2017.

Cindy and Dana Visiting Gorillas in Rwanda, 2017.

CHAPTER 13

A NEW TRAJECTORY

SINCE I HAD MADE the decision to apply to the University for Peace, I noticed an excitement around my daily activities and a magical quality around the mystery that was Costa Rica. Not our verdant, alluring tourist's Costa Rica, but the actual Costa Rica, the country known for peace that provided this unique university.

I didn't know what lay ahead of me. Yet, I knew there was no reversing my commitment. In whatever small, personal way I could manage, I was going to make a difference to bring about a more peaceful world. And I was hoping that quitting corporate and studying forms of practical humanism in Costa Rica, would be the way.

In my daily meditation practice, my heart and mind were open and welcoming of whatever was in store for me. I noticed that my fear had diminished, and I was more trusting of the Universal Spirit of my soul to deliver the best and highest good in my life. During this time, I was consistently gaining physical strength and building my constitution, while visiting the intuitive healer and faithfully following my regimen of Chinese herbs and minerals. I was still on the physical quest to restore my health to the pre-elevator level and was now also seeing a medical doctor who combined his traditional medical training with PhDs in nutrition and psychology.

Dr. Hirschenbein had become so disgusted with the traditional medical model of treating illness rather than preventing illness through wellness that he had dropped out of the healthcare system in favor of his own practice that was more aligned with integrative medicine. He advertised his brand of medicine through PBS segments and health and wellness magazines. It was on PBS that Dana had coincidently seen his program and recognized many of my symptoms in his lecture on gut bacteria. So, Dana carted me off to the integrative medical doctor for more specific testing that could possibly restore my vitality to a healthy-time, long before the elevator incident.

He used sophisticated tests that were only performed in one lab in the United States. His premise was that the quality of uptake of the pre-cursor hormones resulted very directly in the performance of the body's natural chemicals and hormones. His reasoning was that the pre-cursors were the place to solve any root cause issues that would manifest in sub-optimal performance of body functions.

It all made sense to me. Like the intuitive healer, he spent about two hours with me on my initial consultation. *Wow! Somebody else that was interested in my health as much as I was!* And he had valuable knowledge that quickly translated to an additional mineral regimen. Between both healers, I was on my way to physical strength and conditioning that I had not known for over ten years. I began to see this strange illness as a gift to open my eyes to a new career and way of life. I did not know what was next, but I believed that I had the strength and courage to find out.

Conversely, the work front was fraught with equal parts of unimportance and a sense of wasting my time. Knowing that my time in this corporation was limited, I decided that maintaining gratitude for my work colleagues and completing my work tasks to the best of my ability were important to me. Besides, I rationalized that I must perform well to deserve the handsome salary that I received. It was just the right thing to do, in my mind.

After I set about completing the various sections of the UPEACE application, which was due in March for acceptance into the academic year beginning in August of 2004 and ending in July 2005, I reached a stumbling block. In addition to transcripts and application essays, I had to obtain letters from personal and professional colleagues. I would need to identify colleagues to bring into my confidence about my Costa Rica plans so I could request letters of reference from them, despite not wanting anyone to know of my intentions.

Delicately I chose three individuals who had been friends and colleagues for years to share my new calling and request a reference letter. I had been accustomed to writing letters of reference for others, but I had never asked anyone to write a letter for me. I chose three dear friends that were important to me and knew me extremely well—and whom I could trust with my secret agenda: Denny Stone was a peer, colleague, and also my supervisor, at one point. Elizabeth Espinosa was a dear friend and employee—and at one juncture, a business partner. Dr. Kathy Hearn was my spiritual leader, and subsequently a client who hired me for leadership development and organizational development in her role as Spiritual Leader for the World Headquarter of The Centers for Spiritual Living. Each of them wrote the most beautifully articulate and on-point letters I had ever read. They touched my heart so deeply that I cried as I read each of them. I mused that I should have asked for letters earlier in my career to get in touch with my own brilliance.

I submitted the application package, which included my application essay. I then anxiously waited for the response from the committee. I was strongly attached to being accepted to UPEACE and moving to Costa Rica. And that attachment made it more difficult to be at work. The imposter syndrome was taking on a new face.

One assignment I was given after returning to work was as an account executive for the operational teams at the company's large aerospace clients, Lockheed Martin and Hughes. My role was to ensure my team was serving the client on everyday computer operations such as the help desk, network services, and hardware breaks and fixes. These were, generally speaking, all the computer services that would keep the company going behind the scenes. These were the kinds of services that became utilitarian in that all users expected their computers to work all the time.

The only time my team heard from customers was when there was a problem. Since they rarely received accolades from customers, I doubled my efforts to encourage my team and congratulate them when things went well and didn't break. Computers could do strange things and be non-functional quickly. Because I knew my team worked diligently at sometimes boring tasks, I was infuriated when thirty days prior to the end of our fiscal year my vice president insisted that we step up our billing hours on all accounts. She scheduled a conference call to review the billing hours spreadsheet she had taken the liberty to prepare for my four fellow managers and me. The report was sorted by the number of hours each employee should bill by the end of the year and how many hours were remaining to be billed by each employee.

Our vice president was a pleasant woman, but had been given promotions beyond her capabilities and was now simply a go-between to the president. She had become the president's henchman and strictly followed his orders with no critical thinking about why and how to execute the orders. Nor was there any room for discussion between her and the president. Therefore, she was an excellent soldier and carried out his orders even when they made little to no sense.

She began with the team that I had inherited that month and drew my attention to the report that showed 20 of 200 employees that were 400 or more hours behind on billing hours this year. I asked if there were any special circumstances, such as maternity leave, extended illness, or sabbaticals that could account for the low billings. Neither she nor my other colleagues knew the answer to the question.

There was another group of about 100 employees on my report who were about 150 hours behind their billing goals for the year. This didn't sound right to me. Over 50% of my team was behind on their billing hour goals? So I asked, "How were the billing hour goals set at the beginning of the year? Were they realistic for these customer accounts? Did the employees participate in setting them?"

Our VP simply said, "We are way past that. We need you to solve the billing hours issue and get all the team members to their goals by month-end."

"Twenty people could not physically make up 400 hours and bill the 130 hours for March, even if they worked twenty-four hours a day for the next thirty days," I explained.

"I expect you to solve it." She then moved on to harass each of the other four managers in much the same way. There was no dialogue or problem solving, simply outrageous demands to achieve impossible results.

After the call, I investigated why twenty of my newly assigned 200 employees were so low in their billing hours. The explanations were logical and I thoroughly documented the reasons in an annotated report to the vice president. She never acknowledged receipt of my email, nor talked with me about it. Instead, she conducted three more scolding sessions, one per week for the remainder of the month, explaining how my managerial colleagues and I "just did not understand the implications of missing our billing hour goals!"

I wondered how a profit goal could drive an otherwise smart person to so convincingly assign us tasks that were physically impossible and then truly believe the extra ranting and raving would somehow produce the desired result. In my mind, I had crossed the line. I now officially hated business, and it was clearer than ever that I had made the right decision to quit corporate and apply to the University for Peace. It felt so deceptive to be in a job and a role for which I was no longer committed. I was accustomed to giving my whole heart, so I felt a bit like an actor. I was more conflicted than ever.

Nearly everything that now happened in the work setting I gathered as evidence that my view of multinational corporations was accurate. They sucked the life out of people, and used up all the energy and good nature of well-meaning people that had committed themselves to an ideal, for corporate values that were well-intended, but were incongruent with the actions of the leaders, all in favor of profit.

The three corporate values that my management team violated regularly were:

- "we value innovation,"
- "we make decisions with facts," and,
- "we honor teamwork."

I saw no evidence of any of these values in action. The quarterly business reviews (QBRs) were the most publicly humiliating events at CSC. QBRs were supposed to be a data-driven and sometimes anecdotal snapshot into the areas for which the vice presidents were accountable. Then, after all fifteen VPs completed their reports, the second half of the agenda was for the management team to discuss the next quarter priorities. This was to be the top business focus that would require teamwork and innovation over the next quarter.

How it really worked was that VPs would make presentations that involved many facts, did not involve dialogue or teamwork, and was followed with merciless grilling by the CEO. The grilling was generally around mundane details that were irrelevant. *How could he possibly think belittling his VPs was building teamwork, let alone building the business?* The management team rarely ever made it to the next quarter priorities and team innovation portion of the agenda. It was tortuous to witness.

One Thursday evening, in the late spring of 2004, my AOL account said, "You've got mail" and it was from the Rector of UPEACE. I contemplated not opening it right away, but was desperate to know if I could escape the humdrum daily torture called my job.

It read: "We have accepted you into the United Nations University for Peace, International Peace and Conflict Studies Master's Program for the 2004-2005 academic year. You will receive follow-up instructions on your preparations and information on what to bring to Costa Rica for your August arrival. Welcome to UPEACE. We look forward to your acceptance and are honored to have a person of your experience and stature in our program. Warmest Personal Regards, Dr. Amr Abdallah."

"Dana," I yelled out from my home office. She ran into the room wondering what all the yelling was about. "I'm in." I read the acceptance letter to her and then grabbed her and swung her around the room.

When I put her down, Dana said with a big smile, "Congratulations, I knew you would be accepted. They would be crazy not to accept you."

In that moment, two opposing thoughts entered my consciousness. *What an amazing partner I have that can be so excited for me.* And then the fear: *I wonder if our five-year relationship is strong enough to withstand a year apart.*

I pushed the thought from my mind for another day. We needed to celebrate, and this event called for a lovely meal out on the town.

Dear Reader,

It's important to be aware of any contradictions within ourselves, the abyss between how we are responding to circumstances and our own values. Equally important is to give voice to the discrepancies between our values and with the organizations where we are interacting. Values Expert Richard Barrett, says, "Who you are as a leader—the values you embrace, and the beliefs you hold—is automatically transmitted to the group you are responsible for through your words, behaviours, and actions." Bringing light to values that are unspoken is the first step to bridging the abyss.

- *What are your values?*
- *Where might you not be acting in accordance with your values?*
- *Where might you be witnessing contradictions in your values and the values, or lack thereof, of your company or organization?*
- *What can be done about it?*

CHAPTER 14

COSTA RICA BOUND

THE NEXT DAY, when I went to work, I felt above the chaos and a little cocky because I knew that I would not be at CSC much longer. I was more cheerful and engaging, although I didn't dare tell them yet that I was leaving. The previous night, Dana and I had discussed when to give notice. Even though I was legally bound to give two weeks, I felt better about giving thirty-days' notice so I could train my successor and give him or her the best possible chance at success in this crazy company. It turned out that I would be giving my notice in just one month. Everything was suddenly moving very quickly.

I called my sister Deb and my mom and let them know I was accepted to UPEACE, and I would be leaving for Costa Rica in August. Always a big supporter of my ideas, my sister was elated. Mom worried that there could be violence in a foreign country and feared for my safety. I explained where Costa Rica was located and that they didn't even have an army because they stood for peace. I think she was satisfied for the moment.

While I held my decision close, I decided to share my acceptance to UPEACE with the three colleagues and friends who wrote my reference letters. They may have been instrumental to my acceptance. They were all excited about my quitting corporate and envious of my adventuresome spirit.

My colleague, Jeff, had been a consultant and a road warrior for eighteen years. Yet, he and his wife maintained a healthy marriage while she was in Boston and he was in San Diego. I decided to take him into my confidence and ask him the key to staying connected. He said, "It is simple. Talk every day and make the moments that you are physically together important and special."

That night I shared my worry with Dana and my discussion with Jeff. We quickly agreed that our relationship was more important than the geographic separation. Dana would come down with me on the initial trip to set up house and get a lay of the land. And we would talk every day on the phone. Then every six to eight weeks, depending on the school schedule, either Dana would come down to Costa Rica or I would fly home. This way we could maintain our intimate connection, as well. With a plan in place, I knew in my soul that this was an adventure I had to take!

Then, I needed a place to live. I had received information from UPEACE that described living on campus. They only had a few casitas and it seemed a bit too isolated for me. Searching online maps, I saw that Ciudad Colon was 25 kilometers west of San Jose, the capital of Costa Rica. The school was another 10 kilometers west of Ciudad Colon, high in the mountains amid the coffee plantations. Ciudad Colon sat at the base of the mountains and had a population of 2,000 residents and welcomed the students of all races, speaking many more languages than Spanish and English. The students spent money in the town and were always seen walking in groups on the streets.

I looked up rentals in Ciudad Colon. I planned on getting a bike, but not a car, so I needed to be within walking or biking distance to the central part of Ciudad Colon where I would shop and catch my bus to UPEACE each day.

And then I found it: a "casita on the finca," a little house on a 35-acre farm that was surrounded by tropical plants that were house plants in the U.S. It would be available beginning in August and could be rented for the entire year for $450/per month. It came with a housecleaner who would clean weekly and also do my laundry. It was located two kilometers from the center of town that seemed like a perfect walk each day.

Sharon, the owner, explained that she and her husband had moved from Boston and enjoyed their time in the mild weather of Costa Rica. They had bought the 35-acre finca with their three-bedroom home and the additional little one-bedroom, one-bath casita that was about 600 square feet. The little house had a screened-in porch on one side that looked out to the secondary rain forest. She attached a few pictures showing the casita, the porch and a couple of pictures inside the casita. After sending off the deposit, I was locked in!

Done!

From the very start, this trip to Costa Rica proved to be very different from our past vacation. I had expected that, but the drastic surprises were yet to be revealed. The difference rested, perhaps, on the difference between fantasy and real life, between vacation and vocation.

We landed in the new reality—the off-tourist season. Wet and moldy dirt was the overwhelming aroma as we deplaned in San Jose, Costa Rica. The warm rain was pouring in buckets and the sky was pitch black. Unlike landing in a United States airport, which generally provides the shelter of a covered jet way, at the San Jose airport, one walked down a set of portable stairs smack onto the open tarmac. On this day, that meant Dana and I, clinging to the banister, descended in a blinding warm rain and were instantly soaked to the skin by the torrents, as we waded across the tarmac. As we entered the doorway into the airport building itself, seeking baggage claim, we left a trail of water that sloshed from our shoes and dripped from our clothes. I felt as if someone could wring me out and fill a ten-gallon pail.

Dana looked at me and said, "Welcome to Costa Rica. Your new home for a year!"

I laughed. "Like Helen Keller said, 'Life is either a great adventure or nothing!'"

Dana and I claimed our several bags of luggage that contained everything I thought I would need in Costa Rica for a year, before moving through customs to stamp our passports. The customs officer smiled and looked up from my passport and said, "Bienvenida a la Costa Rica y Universidad Para la Paz," as he spotted my year-long visa to attend school. His acknowledgement of my attending the university and generosity warmed my heart, and I forgot my wet clothes and shoes. On prior trips, I did not remember feeling welcomed or unwelcomed anytime I had come through customs in the U.S., just part of the business process that was void of feeling and human connection.

While I understood the customs officer's Spanish, talking to the taxi driver was much more challenging. My Spanish was much worse than I remembered, even after two years of high school Spanish and growing up ten miles from the Mexican border. *Something for me to work on!*

After staying a night at a hotel in San Jose, we rented a car and drove twenty miles to the rented casita. It had stopped raining and was now sunny and humid. The Costa Rica weather pattern was not yet obvious to me. Soon, I discovered that during the rainy season, April to October, the mornings would be sunny and warm, around eighty degrees and humid, but then the clouds would roll in and the torrential rains would take over every afternoon. The evenings might be clear. From December through February, there would be absolutely no rain. Every day would be sunny and 80-85 degrees. November and March were the shoulder months that could be windy, rainy, or dry.

As Dana drove our rental car cautiously down the narrow, steep, and muddy driveway to the finca, I exclaimed, "This is just beautiful. Look at the plants. They look like the same plants that we grow indoors at home."

"More colorful and vibrant," Dana said. She was, after all, the gardener.

And then, there it was: the casita, as advertised and pictured. A sweet little bungalow, with wide square windows, set almost like a fairy tale cottage against the jungle foliage. This was the cocoon I had longed for all my life.

"I can't believe it is right on the edge of the rainforest. I wish I was living here for a year!" Dana cried out.

"Thank you," I said, with tears in my eyes. I was painfully grateful for the opportunity to be here and aware of her selflessness in this decision. I knew, too, that I had to make this work—and in doing so it would be worth it for both of us.

We unloaded the suitcases and walked into the casita and had our first surprise—the "fully furnished" picture that I had was drastically different from the sparse reality.

The worn sheets, linens, scratched pots and pans were very used and not exactly what either Dana, nor I, had in mind for my year in Costa Rica. I think the word is "rudimentary"—and not a comfortable rudimentary at that.

The mattress was made of foam, ranging in thickness from 2-4 inches, depending on which side of the bed you were on, supported by the improvised bed frame loosely constructed with a piece of plywood held up by randomly located bricks. Unfortunately, the bricks did not reach the plywood in many spots. It was the kind of bed a prisoner might have while serving time. No way were we going to try to sleep on that. The next day, we went shopping and found The Price Club warehouse store, similar to Costco. I joined instantly and we set up my little casita to my higher standards. In addition to the usual household items, we bought a miracle dense foam mattress. Dana and Jose, the neighborhood handyman, worked on the brick arrangement and voila' I had a bed that worked very well.

I loved that Dana helped set up the casita with me. The geographical distance from San Diego to Costa Rica was diminished knowing that she would know precisely where I was and could picture me each day when we spoke on the phone.

That first week, Dana and I quickly established a daily routine. We rose at 5:30 a.m. and sat on the porch with our good strong coffee, looking out at the second growth rainforest in the morning. I soon noticed that I was excited to get out of bed and didn't even need an alarm.

Between lounging, we shopped for remaining household items, explored the area, and dined in the local eateries. We became adept at holding an umbrella while loading our purchases into the car, and we continually talked about the beautiful vegetation. The moldy earth smell was replaced by the scents of flowers and aromas of coffee.

The surroundings were bright green compared to San Diego, which is arid and sees six inches of rain a year. I was reminded of the shining tree, and one night when we were sitting on the porch I shared with Dana that this was a time of magic, "I plan to take full advantage of the opportunity to learn and discover my new career while living here."

Costa Rica means "The Rich Coast," and it is an abundant place, the perfect country to be generous enough to donate the 741 acres for a University for Peace. It is unique in its beauty, bordered by two seas—the Caribbean and the Pacific. Within the country are rain forests, "jungle," and many areas unaltered since their creation and inhabited by exquisite rare species of birds. I hoped that with any luck, Dana, during her visits, would spot a scarlet macaw or a wattled bellbird or maybe even the keel-necked toucan. There are also the reptiles—world's fastest lizards—and the startling red eye tree frog.

It didn't take me long to realize that Dana and I were not the only inhabitants of the cute casita: bats slept comfortably upside down from the rafters and swift spiders crossed the ceiling, too. Not to mention, the enemy I found later in my stay: a black potentially fatal-stinging scorpion.

This was Eden, all right, with all its pluses and minuses. The great plus was that Costa Rica was devoted to peace. In 1949, the country had abolished its army. Its record on human rights was sixth in the world, which implied a kind-hearted people.

And that's what really captivated me.

Dear Reader,

Principle #7 refers to "Choose to Be Unstoppable." With any change, even those changes we choose, the transition isn't always smooth. There is often an upward trajectory that can create periods of self-doubt, cause us to question our decisions, and perhaps even quit. According to The Success Principles *author, Jack Canfield, considerations, fears, and roadblocks "are simply part of the process [of change]" and we need to "treat them as what they are—just things to handle—rather than letting them stop you."*

- *How do you approach concerns regarding new situations, even those you welcome?*

- *How do you overcome the self-doubt, fears, considerations, and obstacles that appear?*

- *What could you do differently in responding to future change?*

CHAPTER 15

TIME TO HIT THE BOOKS

THE UNIVERSITY TURNED out to be more grounds and spectacular views than structures. Outside were flags representing all the UN member nations and a sculpture of a dove. The campus could not have been more beautiful or serene.

As I wandered to the cafeteria, I came upon a throng of people from around the world speaking in different languages, many I didn't recognize. This cafeteria was the best bubbling melting pot I had ever entered, and within seconds, I was a member of the global community. On this orientation day, everyone was laughing and talking in generally good spirits. I went to a table and joined a woman, who looked American, and introduced myself. Her name was Tory, and she turned out to be my best friend and buddy through the year at UPEACE. Tory appeared to be in her early thirties, and though she was small, her 5' 1" frame was totally fit, as she was a runner and also regularly practiced yoga. She was married, from Jackson, Wyoming, and a brilliant writer. She told me that she came to school to learn a multicultural curriculum that she could take back to the states to broaden the discourse in public education. Later, I would come to appreciate how well Tory could convey complex issues on paper in a way that all people could understand.

During orientation, we found out there were ninety-two new students chosen from the over 300 applicants. The incoming class represented thirty-seven countries. One quiet African man around thirty-five years old, who I later would get to know very well and who would become my major ally, stood out. From Rwanda, Alphonse was dark-skinned with glasses, bookish, reserved, and only spoke if spoken to. He had a big, bright smile, wore jeans, collared shirt, tennis shoes, and was a moderate Hutu and genocide survivor. Alphonse always spoke in terms of "before" and "after" in Rwanda; here, he was referring to the infamous bloody Civil War, the Rwandan Genocide of 1994, the massacre of the Tutsi and moderate Hutu by members of the Hutu majority. During the approximate 100-day period from April 7 to mid-July 1994, an estimated 800,000 Rwandans were killed, constituting as much as 70% of the Tutsi and 20% of Rwanda's total population. The genocide was planned by members of the core political elite known as the Akuzu, many of whom occupied positions at top levels of the national government. Perpetrators came from the ranks of the Rwandan army, the National Police (*gendarmerie*), government-backed militias, and the militant Hutu civilian population.

Alphonse was so gentle. It was painful to know he had witnessed such horrors and, in fact, had almost been massacred himself. He was a devoted husband and father of two young boys who were back in Rwanda. He wanted to be a university professor for peace and conflict resolution.

I noticed another African man who would also become a major ally. Patrick from Uganda, who was thirty-five, but of slighter build, only 5'3" was an educated man with very dark skin who wore oversized shirts, pants, and shoes. He immediately impressed me as outspoken, bitter, and confrontational about privilege. He worked in refugee camps and was outraged about conditions in Uganda, the brutal Lord's Resistance Army, the nineteen-year civil war, and the conditions in the camps. He was tired of being in the underclass and wanted something better for his people. He would frequently play the devil's advocate in discussions, but we all soon knew he was more of an angel.

Petrina was a blonde, middle-aged woman, another mature student from Iceland, 5'4" tall, married, and the mother of a college-aged daughter; she was pragmatic, smart, and a great listener.

I would come to have only one major antagonist, and I didn't realize it when I first saw him. Abelardo Brenes was a 6'3" Costa Rican who slightly hunched over and spoke in hushed tones. He claimed to be a Buddhist and did not communicate very well. He also displayed a lack of appreciation for strong women, which was a problem for the women students in my program. Abelardo was a professor and the Department Chair of Peace Education.

The student body reflected the United Nations, as we represented:

- North America: U.S., Canada, Mexico
- Latin America: Costa Rica, Brazil, Uruguay, Ecuador, Venezuela, Columbia, Peru
- Western Europe: UK, France, Italy, Iceland, Norway, Finland, Switzerland
- Eastern Europe: Hungary, Romania, Bosnia, Czech Republic
- Middle East: Israel, Lebanon
- Central Asia: Tajikistan, Pakistan, Turkistan, Uzbekistan, Kyrgyzstan
- Pacific Asia: South Korea
- Africa: Ethiopia, Nigeria, Sudan, Togo, Uganda, Cameroon, Tanzania, Kenya

The interesting perspectives I would learn were offered because of this great diversity—55% of our class was from developing countries and only 45% from developed countries.

The degree plan was based on a very intensive approach. We took one course for three weeks at a time, and attended class five days a week from 9:00 a.m.-noon. Every Wednesday afternoon from 2:00-4:00 p.m. a seminar for Peace Education was held which was my emphasis. The world-renowned and accomplished professors flew in to teach the three-week course and make themselves available to students in less-formal settings as well. Groups gathered on the lawns and strolled the trails.

The first course was "The Foundation Course in Peace and Conflict Studies" that all ninety-two students were required to take. We studied and expanded the definitions of peace, conflict, sustainable development, economic globalization, gender dimensions, violence, human needs, human rights, poverty, international law, ethnicity/race/religion, and peace education. I think the bottom line for me was that you can't just speak of peace and conflict as independent variables, but as how they relate to all other issues affecting the world. For example, economic globalization is good for most of the world, but it is not so good for people that live in countries where their human rights or the environment are not protected. The reason it is so important to truly understand the issues, their history, their relationships, etc. is that when an intervention is proposed, we want to ensure we are not exacerbating an already damaging situation. We really want to make sure that the actions that are taken are going to have the best upside potential and can mitigate the downside risks. (My words, not theirs. You can take a woman out of the business, but you can't take the business out of the woman.)

After the first month, I was gaining clarity about how my decades of experience in the corporate world, blended with my new knowledge, might be put to good use in the world after graduation. Conflict management, mediation, and teaching really appealed to me. I was intrigued by the possibilities of bringing value to people and situations that needed help. With so many people asking for help, there was no real reason to go into areas that people don't want assistance.

I soon found opportunities right at school. The University for Peace was compiling course packets (curriculum, videos, materials, etc.) for distribution to other universities in the world. The government of Nigeria had requested the materials and the Nigerian Minister of Education had made three peace courses mandatory in their fifty-two public universities beginning in the 2005-2006 academic year. This was to impact 700,000 students per year in Nigeria, alone. If this plan worked well, other countries were on the list to receive materials.

I received permission from the UPEACE Rector to see the strategic and business plans for implementing this project. I asked clarifying questions, made recommendations, and redlined the plans for the heightened effectiveness. I was hoping to write my thesis in such a way that I could fill one of the resource gaps that the school may have had, while satisfying my academic requirement at the same time. If there was a match, I might be able to build upon that for my next career. And as if on cue, the universe continued providing clues to point me in the right direction.

Early one Sunday morning, I breathed deeply the clean and fresh air that the night's rain had created as I began walking up the long driveway to my new Spiritual Center for the year. The vibrant colors of the bushes were oranges, yellows, purples, and the deep green that is only present with buckets and buckets of rain. It was just beautiful, and I flashed on the shining tree for a moment and knew again I was in the right place at the right time. I found people seated around a covered patio drinking coffee and having sweet treats as they prepared to move into the sanctuary for their Sunday morning service. I immediately noticed they were Americans and Europeans. Ex-pats, I imagined, sprinkled with a few Hispanic men and women.

I poured a cup of coffee and introduced myself to a few people and shared that I was attending the Peace University down the road. They welcomed me and asked about my background. I proudly announced, "I have quit corporate and the profit-only motive and am in search of my next career."

Several people resonated with my proclamation and shared they had either quit or retired from their corporate career in the States or in Europe to lead a more relaxed and peaceful life.

I asked, "Why Costa Rica?"

The man named Haimo, from Germany, said, "Because the country disbanded their army in the 1940s, the Ticos are a peaceful people, and much more laid back than the so-called industrial nations. That is the energy in which I wish to live my life." I sure understood that and was already feeling peaceful in this mystical setting. I could tell I was with my people.

The bells then rang and we were ushered into the forty folding chairs in the converted garage that was beautifully decorated with peaceful pictures, images, and words. I rested into my chair with a fullness and a knowing that I was where I needed to be in my life. I had no idea what was next, but I knew in that moment that everything would be all right, and the future would be revealed a piece at a time.

In the meditation portion of the services, my concerns rose about knowing my school thesis topic. It seemed to be a topic of conversation from the very first week of school, and we were often reminded of it in each of our classes. Other students had come to school already knowing what they wanted to research and study. I felt nervous that I didn't know my thesis premise and asked Spirit for guidance as I sat in the little Unity Church in Piedades.

When I opened my eyes, Rita Marie was standing in front of me. Just by looking at her, I knew she was a force to be reckoned with and I loved it. Originally from Oklahoma, she spoke with a slight southern drawl, and her red hair bounced as she made an announcement that the teachers of the Peace Army would be meeting on Tuesday night to talk about the next stages of the nonviolent communication (NVC) curriculum. Her bright blue eyes sparkled with enthusiasm.

Hmmm. Could it be a coincidence that she was standing in front of me and that I had just recently learned the NVC model in San Diego with Marshall Rosenburg? No coincidences, just synchronicities, as Deepak had said.

Moving to the porch for more treats and coffee, I found Rita Marie and asked her about the Peace Army. She explained that they were teaching NVC and HeartMath® to grammar school teachers who were then taking the information back to their classrooms and teaching the methods to their students. She was a new-thought Unity minister and had dedicated her life to peace. While kindness exuded from her demeanor, I sensed she would take no prisoners if she was determined to get something done—and I soon learned this to be so true.

I shared my corporate background with her and that I was interested in focusing on more than profit motive in organizations. I told her about my need to find a thesis topic for UPEACE and wondered if we could meet to discuss a way I could assist the Peace Army while developing my thesis. She had a gleam in her clear blue eyes, and we set up a meeting for a few weeks later. I think she had something in mind, and I could not wait to find out how this was going to work out.

Dear Reader,

This chapter really calls for us to learn how to create a new rhythm gracefully in completely new situations! I needed my bed and to connect with the people at school and in my new neighborhood. Stepping outside our comfort zone is necessary to grow, and we can do that safely with daily disciplines and rituals that make us feel "at home." Instead of white knuckling your way through change, consider looking at new situations as an opportunity for adventure.

- *Where have you found yourself in new situations?*
- *What disciplines or rituals did you use or could have used that would have made the adjustments easier to make?*
- *What did you discover about yourself along the way?*

CHAPTER 16

OPENING MY EYES

MY PHYSICAL STRENGTH and stamina were at an all-time high. I felt even better than before I fainted in the elevator. Taking stock of my situation, I realized I had not only developed healthy habits, I was successfully maintaining them.

Meditation was a daily habit, and I was walking to and from the bus stop each day. This was about a 15-20-minute walk depending on how many people I spoke with along the way. I was eating fresh vegetables, fruits, eggs, and hormone-free chicken. I had also abandoned gluten, sugar, cow's dairy and white flour. I was relatively stress-free and enjoying my newfound surroundings. Life was again full of intrigue, learning, and joy. While I missed Dana like crazy, I felt solid in our relationship and loved.

My morning ritual brought with it contentment. I would awaken with the sunrise and not need an alarm clock. This was very different from home. I could not remember the last time I jumped out of bed to meet the day when working 7:00 a.m. to 7:00 p.m. I meditated for twenty minutes and set out my college clothes, usually shorts or jeans and a blouse, before I headed to shower. The Jones of New York outfits were safely in the closet in our San Diego home. For breakfast, I dined on a combination of eggs, vegetables, oatmeal, beans, tortillas, and fruit. Each week I would purchase a watermelon, pineapple, or papaya and eat it all week. Dana would call at 8:00 a.m. my time and 6:00 a.m. San Diego time to chat for about fifteen minutes. We generally discussed what had happened the day before and what we both had scheduled for the day. Jeff was right. It was a wonderful way to stay connected in our geographically dispersed worlds.

Then, I would walk up my steep driveway and pass by the cemetery and several blocks of houses on the way to the bus stop for my twenty-minute bus ride through the hills and coffee farms to UPEACE. Usually, many of my colleagues had already arrived and were talking in little groups. Interestingly, the Africans would be standing in the shade and everyone else in the sun. When Dana and I went to Africa in 2002, I remembered how hot the sun was and how little shade there was on the plains. I chuckled to myself as I imagined my African friends wondering what crazy reason could possibly have people standing in the hot sun. This morning was no different, and when I spotted Patrick, I asked if I could sit next to him. "Tell me about yourself," I said to him.

"I work in the refugee camps that have been formed by the nineteen-year civil war in Uganda," he said with a resigned and tired voice. "The Lord's Resistance Army (LRA) is an extremist rebel group from Sudan that burns the houses of my people and kidnaps the children. The boys become child soldiers and the girls become sex slaves. So, the families leave their homes and go to refugee camps before that happens, to protect their families." A pained expression crossed his face.

"I go to the refugee camps to teach peace-building and conflict resolution because there is no real infrastructure," he continued. "Everyone needs a place to live, education, and work. That is hard to do in refugee camps. It would be better if they could all go home, and there was no longer the threat from the LRA. But that doesn't seem possible at this point."

I listened with tears in my eyes at atrocities I had never even heard about. And to be hearing this from a man that had been experiencing this and witnessing it firsthand was a little more than my heart could take. "Thank you for sharing that with me, Patrick. I am hopeful for you and your people that life will get better," I shared with compassion and depth of emotion I didn't know was inside me.

That same week we began studying human rights. We distinguished the difference between crimes (an individual against another or others), human rights violations (a nation-state against another or others), war crimes (during a conflict or war, an individual committing a crime), crimes against humanity (systematic crimes by the nation-state against others) and genocide (intent to annihilate a culture, race, or gender by mass killing). In my seemingly safe American frame of reference, I had not ever really heard or comprehended these topics and definitions. I understood why it is so much easier to pretend it doesn't happen or to occupy ourselves with other things to distract us from seeing and feeling these things in our heart. Images of the atrocities haunted me.

The uplifting part of the studies was about all the well-intending people that were contributing to stop these gross violations. There were millions of people devoting their time, their money, and their know-how, in the short-term, to stop this violence and, in the long-term, to systematically affect their region to prevent this from happening in the future. It is this "human spirit" of kindness, concern, nurturing, and conscience that I was really drawn to—this divine nature in human beings I wanted to continue to develop in myself and to nurture in others. I should have been born ten years earlier because I think I would have fit in quite nicely with the Civil Rights Movement of the sixties.

Not too long into my stay, I awoke at 5:00 a.m. on a Friday morning with the most excruciating pain in the lower left side of my stomach. I had never experienced this kind of intensity. After about two hours of writhing in pain, I called Sharon, my landlady who was also a medical doctor. She showed up in ten minutes with her medical bag and thermos of coffee. After a brief exam she said, "Good news. You're going to live."

I couldn't help but laugh, even though I felt poorly.

"It's one of two things: either you have a kidney stone or something inflaming your intestines, like food poisoning." She observed me for about forty-five minutes while she told me various stories and sipped her coffee. In the meanwhile, Dana called for our regular morning call. "I'm going to stand right here while you tell Dana what is going on with you." Sharon crossed her arms and I knew she meant business.

I told Dana everything that had happened, and as you can imagine, she was quite concerned. Despite her busy schedule, she said she would phone me every few hours to check on me. I hung up and looked to Sharon. "Do you really think I'm going to recover from this?"

"Of course. However, if it would make you feel better, we could transport you to the hospital. I just don't think it's necessary," she said, as she checked my pulse and probed my stomach. "I could take you to the main house and keep an eye on you for the day."

It didn't take long to decide that I'd be more comfortable in my own miracle foam bed, and Sharon left, promising to check in on me. She had no sooner stepped out of the door when the phone rang. Luce was on the other end of the line. She was about fifty years old, very motherly, and sweet. I met Luce and her four lady friends as I was walking home from church three weeks before. I was asking them where I could catch the bus. They spoke only Spanish and I spoke elementary Spanish. By the end of the conversation, I knew the location of the bus stop, and Luce insisted that I join them for a refreshment at her house before I caught the bus. I declined, but she grabbed my hand and off we went to her house, right next to the bus stop. She brought out Coca-light for everyone. The ladies asked me questions about why I was in Costa Rica, about UPEACE, and what I wanted to do. Then her young daughter, Eunice, brought out her English books, and we traded second grade Spanish for me and second grade English for her. Since that time, Luce and I had become friends, and she often checked in on me. When I explained that I was sick, she performed her own diagnosis on the phone. She determined that I had been in the country too long to have the stomach problem that people get in their first two weeks. She promised to bring soup by the next day.

Friday night, neighbor Jose came by to give me the Red Cross ambulance phone number. He volunteered at night driving the ambulance in Ciudad Colon, and he wanted to ensure I knew I could get any help I needed to transport to CIMA, the local state-of-the-art hospital.

On Saturday, my schoolmates, Tory and Arianne, brought everything to make chicken soup. We chatted, ate soup, and then we all took a nap, thanks to the very rainy afternoon making us sleepy. Dana called every few hours to check on me as promised, and she was so happy that the girls were taking care of me.

I reflected on those two days as I sat on the porch in the rainforest on Sunday morning, still not moving well enough to go to church, but eating light foods. I was amazed by the generosity and concern exhibited by Sharon, Luce, Jose, Arianne, and Tory—even though I had only lived in that country for eight weeks and didn't speak the language. I realized that the human spirit was alive and well, and being demonstrated around the world every day in every situation. We are often just too caught up in our own defenses to realize what is all around us, most, if not all, of the time.

Dear Reader,

If we focus on the negative in the news media, we would think that our world will die by tomorrow. We need to broaden our perspective by acknowledging the atrocities in the news, as well as acknowledge that there are good people all over the world engaged in positive endeavors. Here, I refer to Stephen Covey's philosophy of the Circle of Concern and Circle of Influence. When we list our concerns, and identify the ones we can influence and control, we engage with life and take meaningful actions rather than just complain or numb out.

- *What concerns do you have about the world, your community, or your organization?*
- *What are within your control and influence?*
- *What actions can you take that will address these concerns?*

CHAPTER 17

BUILDING MORE CULTURAL AWARENESS

FOR EACH CLASS, I read about a hundred pages a night. At my reading rate of about twenty pages an hour, I spent five hours per day reading, three hours in class, and another three hours writing papers. There really was not a lot of down time, which every now and then led me to be resistant as I didn't get a chance to do the things I wanted to do, like ride my bike, watch a movie, or pleasure read, not to mention spend time with others. It dawned on me that I had successfully recreated my life with all its time management issues right there in Costa Rica. As Jon Kabat-Zinn says, "Wherever you go, there you are!"

I decided to refocus my attention and spend more time with my fellow students. I wanted to find out about their lives, their customs, how they thought and what they felt. It was kind of like an anthropological dig. The key was just to get people to speak up so we could hear and wrestle with the different viewpoints. As we all spent more time together we began to feel more comfortable with each other. Therefore, the things that we would not say to strangers were beginning to be said to each other as friends. I found the interactions to simply be a microcosm of what occurs in the world between cultures.

Our class discussion one day was about economic development in the former Balkan states. The professor said multinational corporations, like McDonald's, have been introduced into Uzbekistan, Kyrgyzstan, Tajikistan, and Turkistan now that they are no longer Soviet States. That began the first firestorm that I had witnessed at the University for Peace.

Kate, a young, vibrant woman from North Carolina blurted out, "Well that might be okay, if it wasn't McDonald's, because they serve food that is bad for you. So, I think that it is really bad that McDonald's is there."

My friend, Muzaffar, a bright, world-savvy person from Uzbekistan yelled out, "Fine, then you go live in Russia and have *no choices* which is what it was like for all those years! Besides, McDonald's gives people jobs!"

Kate retorted, "Yeah, but what kind of jobs, entry-level, minimum wage, not good jobs!"

Muzy was now yelling and pounded the table with his fist, "Those people don't have jobs if McDonald's doesn't come to give them jobs! How do they take care of their families?"

Kate just shrunk back in her chair against this forceful response and pleadingly looked to the professor in a way that was asking him to align with her viewpoint. The professor was deft at giving both views and values their fair airing. I found it fascinating that young Kate had such a narrow U.S.-centric viewpoint and couldn't even hear what Muzy had to say.

This was when I began to see that we are molded by our experiences and culture. And it was from this place that we form our frame of reference that, left unchecked, we believe is the truth, rather than just a viewpoint.

The Kate-Muzy example was an interesting microcosm of the problem that many western governments and NGOs (non-government organizations) have with the work that they do in other countries. Many of them do good work. But when they do *only* what they think is good for the country and the people, they are missing the local viewpoint which is so different from their own. Changes implemented are often worse than the original problem. I guess that is true with any person or organization trying to assist somebody else from only their perspective. I wondered how many times I had unknowingly implemented solutions that created a worse situation than the original problem.

The sociological concept of privilege was discussed in class shortly thereafter. The term is commonly used in the context of social inequality, particularly with regards to race, gender, age, sexual orientation, disability, and social class. It could also extend to economic status although our discussions frequently went towards economic status as the result of access or lack of access. This was not a discussion that we ever had in business school. I didn't quite understand the topic yet. I was a protected class in the U.S. as a woman, over forty, and a lesbian. I imagined therefore that I was not of the privileged class—and soon found out I was wrong.

We had an exercise that was to physically create a human pyramid with the most privileged at the top and the least privileged at the bottom, without speaking. We each adopted a role that included country of origin, gender and title. I drew the wife of a West African President. Other roles were African-American male garbage collector in the United States, female diplomat in France, female child factory worker in India, male farmer in Phillippines, female MBA student in China. Since we could not speak, we would show each other our paper and begin to align ourselves as we believed the hierarchy would go. We rearranged tables and chairs, and all quickly agreed that the least privileged would be lying on the floor under the table.

We quickly determined that the least of us was the female child laborer in India. She had no access, no rights, and was seemingly destined to a difficult life. I was so sad just thinking about her and all the others that were in these roles in the world. The middle section of the human hierarchy was a bit more difficult. There were different viewpoints on what was more valued by the world—being from a particular country or the job title. Most of the African students thought that anybody with any title in the U.S. had more privilege than anyone in Africa. We, Americans, had the opportunity to explain that those in Africa who had titles and education had more access than those in the U.S. without education.

It was becoming more obvious that Americans saw education as the key to privilege, Africans saw country of origin as vital, and Europeans saw title as a place of importance. I recognized the students' viewpoints that were different than my own. I was also enlightened by the plight of others in the world and the ideas of privilege that I had not even heard of until that day.

Then, as we prepared for lunch, we remembered that we needed to choose a class representative—another opportunity to come to understand cultural distinctions. Three nominee names were written on the white board. Each of the three that had been nominated were asked if they would be interested in serving as our class rep should they be selected. Then the vote by a show of hands was conducted. However, as the votes were tallied, it was obvious that our five African colleagues had not voted, let alone nominated anyone. They had, in fact, abstained from the entire process. In the haste to get this task accomplished and get to lunch, most had not even noticed. Several people then realized that we were not yet complete and needed an explanation from our African friends.

Somebody asked, "Why didn't you participate?"

None of them responded. They looked down at their hands in their lap.

"I don't think we should have a class representative that a fourth of the class did not participate in selecting," said one of my peers. Those from North America and Europe were getting impatient and didn't know what to do. They were angry, hungry, and some just wanted to claim the process complete. "They could have participated if they wanted to and they chose not to," added another.

I was getting more and more uneasy. The Peace University was not peaceful in this moment. I suggested we go to lunch and reconvene five minutes before our afternoon class to discuss a possible solution and pathway forward. All agreed, and then I asked my African colleagues if I could have lunch with them. After gathering our food and convening at the lunch table, I asked, "Why did you not participate in the nomination and voting process?"

Alphonse said, "This is just not our way."

Not knowing at all what he meant. I asked, "What is your way?"

Assouan replied, "We can't just ask everyone to speak the names out loud of people being nominated."

"Was there another way to ask for nominations?" I inquired.

Christine said, "Can't we just write a name on a piece of paper and turn it in privately? What if people feel bad by not being nominated?"

"Of course we can," I responded. "Why would that way work better than saying the names aloud?"

We had recently learned about high-context and low-context cultures. I wondered if that was at work here. High-context cultures, such as Africa and Asia, require solving problems and learning in groups. The interpersonal relationships and non-verbal methods are much more important than words when communicating. Trust must also be developed before business transactions can begin.

Conversely, low context cultures can follow a set of described rules to solve problems or work together. The interpersonal relationship and trust may not be necessary in order to conduct business transactions.

Hence, electing governmental representatives in the United States and most European nations was a precise and prescribed manner. For my African friends, they would not elect a representative this way. It felt cold and lacking personal trust to them.

"Who would collect and read the pieces of paper for nominations?" I asked Christine.

"You could do that," she said to me.

I looked at the others at the table and they were all nodding.

I asked, "Because you trust me?"

Patrick said, "Yes, and we know you would not cheat a group of people."

I was moved that I was now a trusted elder in the group. I felt appreciated for who I really was and not for what I could do for someone. This was a whole new feeling for me, and it felt "right" in my soul.

"I will do that for us," I said. "Then what is the next step in the process? Would I announce the nominated people?"

Emmanual said, "Yes, and ask them if they are interested in serving in this capacity."

"I got it. Then, how do we conduct the vote?" I inquired.

Christine said, "Again by private ballots."

"Then, I would count the ballots and announce the winner?" I asked.

"Yes," She replied.

"I think I would not announce any voting numbers. Just the selected person. Right?" I inquired.

"Yes, that is the way," she quietly remarked.

I looked around the lunch table and asked if they would all participate in the process if we conducted it this way.

They nodded their heads and smiled.

I now understood how to accomplish our task. By using this process for the high-context colleagues and slowing down my low-context colleagues with an added explanation and clear process, I believed all would be served, and we would have a class rep within ten minutes.

We all walked back to the classroom and I asked the professor and the students for fifteen minutes to accomplish our class representative selection process. I communicated the process and wrote it on the white board. We tore little pieces of paper for our nomination and voting process. We had eight nominations of which only two were interested in serving. We conducted the private ballot voting and had our new class representative—Christina, from Uganda. Everyone cheered and we moved into our afternoon class.

Real life experiences helped me to apply the teachings from this little liberal arts university in the jungles of Costa Rica. Peace Studies were not always peaceful, I was discovering. Here, I was again in a peacemaker role. And this time it was different. I was no longer coming from a place of fearing for my safety, but was working toward a greater good for the whole. But there was more here. Taking the time to understand somebody else and interject patience into the drive to accomplish the next task was becoming increasingly important and led me to ponder the effect in the business world.

My conclusion was drawn from my past experience: there was just not enough time to listen. Corporations were sucking the life out of people because the employees were looked upon as robots on an assembly line. Do more in less time. This was how money was made, right? Time is money.

I was beginning to think there might just be a better way.

Dear Readers,

When we are with people from different countries, our cultural differences are obvious. However, when we are with people who live in our same country, town, or work in the same organization, the differences are shrouded in our assumptions. The key is to ask more questions before we assume our way is right. Gaining clarity before moving into action is imperative for harmony.

- *What situation might be calling you to come to know someone or a group of people better before creating a plan of action?*
- *What questions do you need to ask?*
- *Where might you be pushing your viewpoint or agenda?*

CHAPTER 18

POWER OVER

CORPORATE BUSINESSES, as I knew them, in the United States were profit driven and rarely had time or interest in acknowledging the people side of the business. People were lucky to have jobs, was the mantra in the eighties. Then, the nineties became an employee's market, and software engineers were in short supply. Suddenly, we were offering signing bonuses and streamlining our hiring timeline to hire more qualified people and get them on the payroll faster and faster. People were a means to an end in business.

The dot-com bust notwithstanding, the economy in the United States was thriving and high-end technical jobs were in abundance in my world. It had not occurred to me that economic development and prosperity was not being enjoyed by people the world over. I, of course, knew there were people that did not make as much money as we did in the U.S., but we also had a higher cost of living in our country so, that somehow seemed to balance out, at least in my mind.

The multinational corporation (MNC) was discussed in our class that month as the problem with a host of economic ills in developing countries. From mining in the Amazon to drilling for oil in Nigeria, to dams for hydroelectricity in China, MNC's were raping and pillaging the land. The people of these countries were trading their long-term livelihood on the land for their short-term earnings that were offered by the MNCs in exchange for cheap labor. Or, at least, this was how the narrative went in our discussions and classroom debates.

The definition of an MNC is that of a business that sells goods or services in many countries. Therefore, the legal and moral obligation is not to one country with the proper safeguards, but instead it is a "stateless actor" with a large potential for conflict of laws.

While my time at UPEACE was my first exposure to multinational corporations as a descriptor, essentially, I had just resigned from an MNC that worked in many countries and was not running around breaking the law or taking advantage of inexpensive labor. However, I did remember outsourcing computer programming to a company in India in the late 1990s and early 2000s. I was astonished at the venomous discussions at UPEACE about MNCs and wanted on more than one occasion to interject some reality to the discussions. However, my thoughts were not fully formed so I just listened. As I was reading more articles and doing more research on the examples that were given, I could not confidently argue against the information I read.

The next day in class we discussed the United Fruit Company, an American corporation that traded in tropical fruit, mostly bananas grown in Central and South America. The lecturer explained that this was a prime example of exploitive neocolonialism by an MNC with an unhealthy influence on the internal politics of Guatemala, Honduras, and Costa Rica.

Furthermore, he explained the environmental degradation, union-busting, and worker exploitation to a level that sounded like slavery to me. I was stunned and realized this was another set of horrific practices that I had not yet been exposed to, and was still struggling with understanding the economics of the banana industry.

We moved into a subgroup exercise to determine how the retail price of ten cents would be divided amongst all parties that touched the banana between growing a banana and a consumer purchasing it in a grocery store in the United States. Our guesses were all over the place in our subgroup. We could all agree that the grower would get a small amount, maybe two cents. The retailer would get a little more, maybe three cents and the MNC that purchased, transported, and distributed the banana would get the largest share of the ten cents. Maybe five cents.

Boy, were we off base!

It turns out that the grower gets 1/10 of a cent, the retailer gets ½ cent and the MNC gets the remaining nine+ cents of the ten-cent banana paid by the consumer. I was shocked, and I could not wait to share this newfound information with Dana.

As was our custom, on Sunday afternoon we would talk on the phone for an hour or so. We discussed everything going on in our respective lives in San Diego and Costa Rica, including our respective Unity Church experiences that morning. We always saved time for me to share what I had learned from class that week.

"You are going to be stunned when I tell you about multinational corporations."

"Did you talk about the United Fruit Company?" she asked me.

"How did you know?" I was stunned.

"They are the poster child for exploitation of workers, the land, and the worst practices in global businesses," she said calmly.

Here, I thought I was going to share all this new information and she already knew it. "Well, I bet you didn't know that the growers only receive 1/10 of a cent on a ten-cent banana," I shared with new important knowledge.

"No, I didn't, but I am not surprised," she offered.

"How did you know about MNCs and the United Fruit Company?" I asked in awe.

"You forget my undergraduate degree is in liberal arts with an emphasis on race, ethnicity, and gender, and we had a broad array of classes and books on socioeconomic plights in the world. Of course, it was the seventies and eighties so we were learning about the shortcomings of democracy with Watergate and such," she explained.

"How could I not know?" I asked with genuine surprise.

"You went to business school and then on to get an MBA in Information Technology. You learned it well, but it is just a narrow slice of the world," she replied softly.

My notion of self as a well-informed and compassionate global citizen was shattered. I wondered what else I didn't know about life, humanity, and the workings of our world to be the well-informed and committed global citizen I wanted to be. Luckily, I had chosen the right place to correct that—and the lessons continued.

African colonialism piqued my curiosity due to my newfound friendships with Alphonse, Patrick, and Christina. It was not a scientific curiosity, but more an interest in wanting to better understand their lives, experiences, and how they saw the world. Alphonse assisted my learning over lunch. He showed me pictures of his family, and I sensed that he missed them terribly. The only way he and his wife communicated was via Western Union telegrams. One son was in school and the other would begin primary education the next year. His wife was pregnant and expecting their third child, who was due before Alphonse would return home next year. My heart once again ached for him. *What commitment and dedication to his calling!*

We had an upcoming project due in our class and I asked him if we could team up to write about the aftermath of genocide and "Gacaca," which literally means "justice on the grass," in his language. It was a citizen-based justice that Rwandans decided to put into place in an attempt to deal with the crimes of the 1994 genocide. It was the Rwandan version of the Truth and Reconciliation Commission still underway in South Africa after decades of apartheid rule.

I didn't think my heart could at all focus on genocide, but talking about justice, mercy, and the human heart after atrocities was at least a possible move forward. I told him that I had recently read that former President Bill Clinton's biggest regret while president of the United States was that he did not intervene during the Rwandan genocide.

He took my hand and looked me in the eye, "Thank you for sharing President Clinton's words with me. It brings me a greater understanding."

We agreed that we would work together to teach our fellow students about Gacaca that was now underway in Rwanda and which was creating a version of justice by off-loading the Rwandan courts of processing hundreds and thousands of crimes—and at the same time was rekindling humanity through forgiveness and mercy.

In the same moment, my heart was filled with admiration for my new friends and colleagues that amidst the atrocities in their lives, they were generous, kind, and compassionate for others. It just didn't seem fair. After learning that I was privileged and that many in the world were at less stature and status than I was, I began to feel guilty for the life that I had and wondered about the good fortune that I had been given to be born into a wealthy nation.

It was not unlike my feelings at ten years old to hear that I would be baptized and would be saved for eternity—and then learning that not all would be saved unless they believed in Jesus Christ. At forty-six years old, I knew that the simplistic religious explanation of my childhood was invalid. However, the guilty feelings of being chosen were difficult to release. In reflection, I realized that I could learn much from this man who described all of his life events as before or after genocide, the horrific marker of his life—a man who was now committed to make a difference. Hearing this, I was convinced that from my place of privilege I could do something, and in doing so, I believed my guilt would subside.

Alphonse and I created a skit where we wrote brief roles for volunteers to play in the Gacaca experience. Alphonse was the primary judge of the Gacaca, I was the narrator of the proceedings, and we had enlisted others to embody the role of family members of those that were allegedly killed by a government soldier. We also had government soldier actors that were being accused of crimes.

The Gacaca, "justice on the grass," is a restorative justice practice that eases the massive backlog of genocide suspects and allows for reparations and community restoration. Alphonse opened the panel with defining the facts of genocide that had occurred in this community across the specific timeframe. He then asked for an accuser to step forward, describe the incident that occurred, and name the accused. A woman began to describe a day that soldiers came into her home, killed her husband while the family watched, and took her son to serve as a child soldier. She described in excruciating detail and accused a man in the audience of being the offender.

Every person in our classroom was crying from heartbreak at hearing the atrocities that were brought on this woman and her family. Our classmates were rapt with attention to hear from the accused. Then, the primary judge asked the accused to come forward and state his name. He was then asked if he had committed these crimes for which he was accused. The man replied that he was and then proceeded to make a full disclosure of the details of the crime he had committed. He ended his confession by naming his accomplices and offering his apology to the woman.

Alphonse, as the primary judge, was able to ask questions to discern the completeness of the confession. He then asked more questions to determine the depth of this man's responsibility. After receiving his answers, he and the other panel of judges discussed the information and decided that the soldier's family was threatened, and he was truly sorry for his actions—and did not act on his own volition. Part of the prison sentence was forgiven, and he was required to serve half of his remaining sentence through community work in the local community. The woman had been given her chance to have her voice heard, and the perpetrator was apologetic and would serve his time for his crimes. Our classmates were moved by the enormity of the crime and the small amount of healing that occurred in the Gacaca process that focused on restorative justice—not on punitive justice.

We all began to understand Alphonse just a little bit more that day.

Dear Reader,

We often exert power over others when we fear our needs won't be met. Power over is an accepted method to accomplish tasks with a lot of people because there is an underlying belief that we can never get everybody on the same page, that it will take too long, and speed is of the essence. This practice inhibits team cohesiveness and the empowerment of others—and possibly the discovery of a better way to reach our goals.

- *How might you be using power over as a defense to something you fear?*
- *How might you choose to respond rather than react?*
- *What might healthy responses be to some of your challenges?*

CHAPTER 19

NEITHER HERE NOR THERE

———————————

WHEN WE WERE ABOUT a third of the way through the school year and learning about research in preparation for our master's thesis, I received some guidance on how to frame my thesis on the Peace Army of Costa Rica and submitted my proposal to Abelardo for approval.

The Peace Army of Costa Rica is a program designed to assist classroom teachers, not only to practice personal and interpersonal skills, but teach students how to use skills to create peaceful situations where otherwise conflict might arise. The program was to seed peace early in one's life, which would enhance the environment of peace throughout families, communities, and spread into the world. The problem was that it was still a pilot program with three instructors in only 400 schools. I knew how to scale this project to have a greater impact and reach more people by imbedding it into the education system and making it a mandatory curriculum.

The program consisted of two skills. One of these skills is the Freeze-Frame Method of the HeartMath® Institute. This is a self-distancing exercise to assist one in disengaging from an emotionally triggered situation so that it doesn't escalate and in fact may be resolved. Using the breath and by focusing on the heart, the idea is to activate a positive feeling, such as appreciation for a person or situation in your life. The next step is to determine what action or attitude is needed to create peace and balance within. The idea is to change your perception about the situation and to sustain it.

The second skill is Dr. Marshall Rosenberg's Nonviolent Communication (NVC). This technique shifts our perception of what other people have "done to us," to what we need in a situation. It's a four-step process where we observe a situation that is unsettling to us. We express our feelings about the situation before moving on to state what we need. Then we make a specific request for concrete actions that is in alignment with our well-being, not furthering criticism or blame. I would soon learn just how valuable these techniques could be and, in essence, practice what I preached.

Professor Abelardo Brenes was a Costa Rican man with a slow and deliberate style that quickly sent me into impatience and frustration the second he began talking. My respect and acceptance of him was decreasing with each course because he did not seem that knowledgeable on the academic material. But the part that was most upsetting to me was that we could not seem to dialogue.

To describe it as two monologues would not be accurate. It was more like a one-sided monologue where he spoke, then I would address his statement. He would then speak again and I would address his statement. Then I would get tired of that non-dialogue, so I would make a statement, and he would respond with a random statement that was on his mind and then tilt his head and smile. He was a practicing Buddhist and would talk in a hushed tone, have the non-dialogue, and then smile all the while. Somehow, he thought that was living the middle way of the Buddhist eightfold path, which is right understanding, right intent, right speech, right action, right livelihood, right effort, right mindfulness, and right concentration. I had difficulty seeing it, and my apprehensions about Abelardo were all too soon verified.

More than once, I had set up an appointment with him to discuss coursework or projects. The same non-dialogue would happen. I would share with him that I didn't feel heard, and he would tell me that I was not being peaceful. If anyone could drive me to non-peace it was him, and I did my best to let it all go. Yet, that *laisse faire* attitude was nowhere to be found the day I received my rejected thesis outline. I was at lunch with my friend, Tory.

I read her the handwritten scribble, "'This thesis proposal is not academically sound.'"

I thought my head was going to blow off. "Academically sound! Are you f'ing kidding me?" I said to Tory.

"I told you he doesn't know what he is talking about. He is not fit at all to be our academic advisor, let alone our professor," Tory exclaimed.

"How can I even talk to him in a calm voice? He is so odd. He doesn't listen, and has a weird way of talking that doesn't make sense, and yet he has complete authority over whether or not we get our degree!" I exclaimed.

By then we were convinced he had a problem with women, something that we had suspected the very first day of the school year. After another fifteen minutes of ranting, we finished our lunch, and she suggested I talk with our Assistant Professor Eliana to figure out how to edit my thesis proposal into an acceptable project. This turned out to be a brilliant suggestion, and in short order, she had helped me modify the thesis as an action research project. The Peace Army of Costa Rica was going to get a strategic plan for scaling to the next level, and I was going to get a thesis. And with Christmas break around the corner, I had a little time to contemplate that and more.

With my December peace and violence course completed with flying colors, I headed home for a three-week Christmas break. While the first half of my studies had gone well, I still wasn't sure if all the pieces of my life fit. My mind and heart were in conflict, and, for the first time since making the decision to pursue my degree, doubts nagged at me and fear had me questioning if I'd be able to accomplish my goal.

In addition to being wildly excited to see Dana, I was eager to reconnect with family and friends. Nearly every person I saw at holiday gatherings asked me about my exotic experience of quitting corporate and going to Costa Rica. It was fun sharing a few experiences with my classmates and describing our growing friendships.

Just once, I disclosed my new knowledge regarding multinational corporations, with Jeff, who immediately began to defend my former company. I had expected him to ask questions and work to understand different viewpoints. I wasn't denouncing CSC, but only hoping to enlarge the viewpoints beyond the strong business narrative in the United States. The reluctance to hear anything different than what he already knew to be true was palpable. Not being one to upset the status quo in a relationship, I decided I would need to be much more selective in sharing the new views I had acquired. I felt like a kitten discovering claws. *How would I effectively use this new information and not unintentionally create a bloody mess of my life?*

Mostly, I engaged with friends and family at the level that was important to them. This was fun, familiar, and comforting to me. Many wanted to know what I was going to do next in my career. I had no answer at all. This was an unfamiliar place to be. With the exception of my illness, in the past, I generally knew where I was going and what was next in my life. Their questions only fueled the fear and doubts that had followed me from Costa Rica.

On the drive home from one holiday dinner party, I shared with Dana the difficulty I was having answering the inquiries from friends.

She asked, "What is tripping you up?"

"I am used to being clear and precise, you know, businesslike. That's how people know me. I feel like I have lost that ability. Or maybe I don't even want to be that person anymore—and I am afraid people will think I am a flake." I was trying to make sense of what I was feeling along with my seeming inadequacy to perform.

Dana again threw me a life preserver as I was flailing in the unknown waters. "Maybe you could say 'I am only half way through my degree and plan to focus on what is next for me in the second semester. What ideas might you have for me?' How does that feel to you?" she asked.

We drove in silence down I-5 for a while before I spoke again. "The truth is, I really don't know what I am going to do. I am scared and worried I won't be able to make a living and contribute to our lifestyle." Tears streamed down my face, "I am worried that you can't count on me! I want to be your rock. Just like you are for me. I feel guilty sometimes, like a taker. You are in San Diego, taking care of our home and your career, and I am flitting about Central America learning about nation states, cultures, peace, and violence. It feels so self-indulgent, like a luxury."

"I would do anything in the world for you. This Costa Rican adventure is what you need to finish healing your body. You look vibrant, healthy, strong, and beautiful. It is working!"

"I agree with all that," I cleared my throat. "But the second semester tuition of $9,000 is due next week. I actually think that since I have gotten everything I went to Costa Rica for, I don't need to go back. I don't think fighting with Abelardo and writing a thesis on the Peace Army are what I need to figure out my new career. I can easily do that from here!" I rationalized.

We had already pulled into the driveway and sat in the car with the engine turned off for this inappropriately timed conversation at midnight.

"And what would you do?" she asked.

"I don't know. Begin putting out resumes and volunteering at non-profits." I offered.

Dana looked at me with incredulousness, "Just stay with it. We already planned the $9,000 tuition. No financial circumstances have changed since you left for school last August. I don't understand where all this is coming from."

"I feel like a princess who is not pulling her own weight," I squeaked out.

"Keep going to school. This is good for both of us," she pleaded.

"Okay," I said, reluctantly, noticing that I was a little pissed off, as I got out of the car and walked into the house.

Was I mad because I felt like a petulant child with a parent that seems to know more than me? Or was I afraid she was right and there was much more to my journey in Costa Rica?

Then I realized that this felt a lot like the time when the president of the company I worked for in my twenties essentially forced me to go to college.

It was time for me to consider why I insisted on creating my own obstacles to things that were obviously meant to help me.

Dear Reader,

There are often times when we are on a journey (think of the Hero's journey) where darkness consumes us, and we want nothing more than to bail out of a situation to resolve the tension. What we don't understand is that this is exactly the time to stay engaged. That's where the creativity arises and where the juices begin to flow. If we can just hold the tension a little longer, the pieces, the next steps, will emerge. It's not for the faint of heart; however, there are rewards. The place of the unknown is where new opportunities present themselves that we might otherwise miss if we're rushing through life.

- *What are those situations where you want to hurry up and get through them rather than be fully present?*
- *Where has your impatience created more problems than solutions in the past?*
- *What do you need to do to be patient with the next transitional phase in your life?*

CHAPTER 20

MAKING PEACE WITH VIOLENCE

THE FIRST CLASS of the second semester, in January of 2005, was The Psychology of Peace and Violence. The professor had flown in from working with the government and people of Indonesia in the aftermath of the tsunami on December 26, 2004. He shared, in vivid detail, the loss of life, how it took days, and sometimes weeks, to discover if family members were alive or dead. Bodies in need of identification had washed up on beaches, in fields, and along roads. Buildings had collapsed and rubble remained as the waters receded. Physical landmarks and rich history were washed away. All of it was difficult to fathom. This was only three weeks after the tsunami and so much was still in flux. The latest death toll was nearing 180,000 people and climbing.

My business mind appreciated learning about the details of setting up refugee camps and organizing distribution of water, food, and supplies from the generous outpouring of humanitarian aid from around the world. My heart ached hearing the stories and nearly every day of this course, I cried. Listening to his descriptions of the tsunami aftermath activated my empathy to such a degree that I knew that I would never be able to use my skills to contribute in situations like these. I'd be in continual emotional breakdown and wholly ineffective. This was a familiar feeling when Alphonse and I had worked together on the Rwandan genocide project the previous semester.

Amidst my thoughts and feelings, the month moved forward at a glacial pace as the professor continued sharing beyond the tsunami experience to his on-the-ground experience with African and South American communities in the most horrific and violent circumstances. He offered his firsthand knowledge of how roving bands of rebels would come into small villages, burn down homes, kill adults, and kidnap young boys and girls. The boys would then be turned into child soldiers, and the girls would be sex slaves for the rebel soldiers. The organization for which the professor worked would rescue the boys and girls and bring them back to their village, engaging the village elders in discovering the appropriate communal ritual to lovingly bring back the rescued child soldiers into the community. This was no easy feat, as sometimes, the young men under threat from the rebel factions had in fact been the very people that killed their parents. Forgiveness and repatriating the child soldiers was a multistep and complicated process.

The young women who were rescued were even more difficult for the community members to accept back into the village. They were seen as unclean, blemished, and not fit to be taken as a wife by a respectable village man. I was so deeply in my own revulsion that I didn't hear the details of the program to repatriate the young women. I had to excuse myself to the bathroom and vomit. I was not ever going to understand this kind of violence. I shielded myself against hearing more, thought of other happier times, and asked a friend to dinner that night to reconnect with something pleasant. I was drowning in my own emotions as images of my childhood and the violence I endured filtered in and around the images of those abducted children. I had to shake myself out of it.

Later that day as I began to cross the street, I looked over my shoulder for traffic and fell in a giant pothole. Startled at finding myself on the ground, I quickly realized there were kind hands reaching down to lift me back to the sidewalk. I sat on the curb for a moment to reassess my twisted ankle and possible severity of the injury. I limped to the restaurant for dinner.

The next morning, my ankle was swollen, discolored, and hurt like crazy. A brief taxi ride to the hospital and x-rays revealed a severe sprain and nothing broken. Rest, ice, compression bandage, and elevation (RICE), was the treatment, the same as the athletic injuries of my youth.

I now had a legitimate excuse to not go to school for at least a week. I probably subconsciously engineered a way to shield myself and my emotions from any further assaults. This experience, however, helped me determine that my heart was not meant to be with people in the most dire circumstances. Being a first responder and providing humanitarian aid would not be my future career. My skills and talents definitely lay elsewhere. And that's what I focused on.

March was the month to make significant writing progress on the Peace Army thesis. My new work space in the apartment was filled with books, printed research, Peace Army curriculum, and other assorted materials I had gathered over the previous four months.

Rita Marie and I had spent hours together over the last couple of months diving into the feedback data from the Peace Army pilot program. We had discussed, investigated, and discerned a few possible paths to scale the Peace Army teachings into all primary schools in Costa Rica.

We agreed that teaching HeartMath® and Non-Violent Communication (NVC) methods to primary school students was the right place to teach these peace building skills. We were not at all clear how we would teach the teachers quickly enough to proliferate these skills and stem the early trends of growing violence in the barrios.

As it was, Costa Rica urban areas did not have enough primary school buildings and facilities to teach the number of school children. Therefore, the Ministry of Education had decided to run three school shifts of three hours each. This meant that a child would be assigned a school shift and the remaining daytime hours they would have no other activities, if their parents worked. They were essentially unsupervised and easy prey for unsavory characters. Gangs, drugs, and violence were increasing as families were migrating from the rural farms to the urban areas for the promise of economic growth and stability. With a deep commitment to bring more peace-making skills to children and their families, I reasoned I could apply my business skills and knowledge of organizations to progress the agenda of this Peace Army program.

One rainy afternoon, Rita Marie shared with me that there had been recent rumblings that Oscar Arias, former president of Costa Rica, was exploring his chances of winning another presidential term. He was much beloved by the Costa Ricans and was the recipient of the Nobel Peace prize in 1987 for a plan designed to put an end to the cruel civil wars that were devastating Central America. The peace plan was approved by Costa Rica, Guatemala, El Salvador, Honduras, and Nicaragua. The primary goals were safeguards for human rights, free elections, and an end to the foreign interference in the countries' internal affairs.

We were excited about the possibilities. We hypothesized that if Mr. Arias ran for president, he would win. Then, we would have a sympathetic ear in his administration and the Ministry of Education to discuss the Peace Army program as a method to teach peaceful communication at the elementary school level. We further imagined making the peace-building curriculum a compulsory requirement in the teacher accreditation degree at the university, much like reading and arithmetic knowledge and skills. Our data from the pilot program was showing promising results with improved grades and decreased fighting and expulsions among the Peace Army students. We could possibly frame this program as a critical component in maintaining a peaceful Costa Rica. This was probably a stretch, but our hearts were in the right place.

I left our meeting that day full of energy and imagination that specific trends and intractable viewpoints could be changed. In fact, a person or a small group of people's interventions was the only action that could impact change. I remembered the quote by Margaret Mead: "Never doubt that a small group of thoughtful, committed citizens can change the world; indeed, it's the only thing that ever has."

And individually, I set to work to complete my thesis.

Rain pounded on the tin roof and the winds howled as I completed the next course's academic paper on the effects of bullying. Chock full of facts and figures, there was mounting evidence that elementary schools in San Diego were experiencing increased taunting and bullying behaviors from one child to another. My research and premise of the paper was that proven programs were implemented and could be replicated to stem bullying between kids.

The lights flickered for the umpteenth time, and then the power went out. This was not uncommon in Ciudad Colon, but very untimely as this evening, I needed to finish writing my reflective paper for this course. Luckily, I had enough juice on my laptop battery to write for another two hours.

As I sat in the dark with the candles lit, I started feeling sorry for myself. I missed Dana terribly, even though I knew that it was only three months until I would be back home. And yet the distance that night was unbearable. As I stared at the flickering candles, I wondered how my new friends dealt with their separations—not only because of school, but of the political climates that often tore families apart—bullying on a grand scale. Once again, it was just too big to imagine. My plight was big enough to handle right then.

The confluence of missing Dana and writing about bullying took me to a place of reflection about my parent's relationship. Up until then,

I had seen them as people that could not get along well. Fighting and physical abuse were so woven into the fabric of my childhood that I had become numb to its effects. I certainly didn't talk about it with people. As I wrote down my reflections, I began to see my dad, the bully, as a man ill equipped to be a good husband or a good father. It must have been very hard for my parents when my dad, the Navy man, would leave the family for six months at a time on a ship heading to the Viet Nam War.

At least Dana and I were able to talk on the phone each day and visit each other every 6-8 weeks. My parents had only letters available to them. *How can you really stay connected that way? How could he profess love in his letters and then within a month of returning home return to his old patterns of yelling, taunting, and beating my mom and, then later, his daughters?* His violence knew no boundaries. I had yet to forgive him, but perhaps by understanding him I could help prevent that behavior elsewhere. I had a glimmer of compassion for him in that moment that quickly gave way to sadness about my family's plight. Then, I flashbacked on the horrific violence that distorted my own childhood.

In the summer of 1967, as a family, we moved to North Chicago, Illinois. My dad would be home every day as he had been assigned "shore duty" to train new naval recruits at the Great Lakes Naval Training Center, essentially boot camp. As company commander, he was charged with the responsibility for training the recruits to be sailors worthy of wearing the United States Navy uniform and preparing them for future naval assignments due to this intense, physical, emotional, and intellectual twelve-week training. That seemed very cool to me and I was proud of my dad for this honor that had been bestowed on him.

I was full of hope to spend more time with him because he would no longer be overseas for six months out of the year. I had also thought that his increased drinking and the escalation in beatings was because he was gone so much and it was so disruptive to the family when he came home.

I pushed my worries aside because I would have my baseball buddy and playmate back! And we'd be close to my Uncle Bill, Aunt Joni, and cousins Paula and Ricky who were also stationed in Great Lakes. We could hardly contain chatter about reuniting with them and all the fun things we'd do together.

Shortly after settling in, my mom went to work at the Navy Exchange, the retail store for the military base. Now all the household chores fell to my sisters and me. I fixed dinner and washed dishes each night. Deb dried dishes and Pam cleared the table and swept the kitchen floor. My mom worked Tuesday through Saturday and was home Sunday and Monday. But household cleaning chores for some reason had to be done on Saturday. You guessed it—the little band of sisters also did the Saturday cleaning chores. I did the family laundry, Deb vacuumed the house, and Pam dusted the furniture.

Our military housing was an old, 1940s-built barracks. It had concrete construction, and minimal windows with the living room, kitchen, and utility room downstairs and extremely steep stairs to the second floor where the three bedrooms and one bathroom were situated.

The stairs were hard to negotiate for my five and six-year-old sisters, but negotiate they did. There was no excuse for not contributing to the family chores. And the sooner we finished, the sooner we could go out and play, me to baseball with the neighbor boys, and Deb and Pam to Barbie's and other games with the neighborhood girls. In the warm summer evenings, we played kick the can with the neighborhood kids.

The promise of more time with Dad was dashed when he decided to take a second job and work evenings and weekends. Looking back, I wondered if they had money issues because I never understood the shift in working circumstances. The family pattern that emerged was Dad coming home drunk after his evening job and yelling at why things were not right in the household or with how my mom was being one way or another or not doing things to his preference—which was ever changing. It was obvious she was never good enough for him.

At least once a week, I would wake up to their yelling and pray they would just stop being so mean to each other. My younger sisters still shared a room and would also wake up during the shouting matches. They began coming into my bed at night, and I would sleep in the middle, hugging them both, and tell them it would all be okay. "Don't worry," I would say to them as I held them or stroked their little foreheads. Sometimes we were caught in the fray. Sunday mornings we would all act like everything was okay.

It was very confusing for me at nine years old to understand how my sisters and I would be punching bags for Dad's drunken rages. I questioned what forces forged a personality. Some children so treated grow up to beat their own. Others become gentler and dedicate themselves to peace. My UPEACE classmates had been through worse violence on a larger scale, and they seemed to move forward with courage. Under the flickering light of my candles and the blue-glow of my laptop's screen, I wanted to be more like my colleagues. They modeled behavior to work with life's challenges as they arrived and could still be generous with others in the process.

Pop, pop, pop. Like marbles dropping, realizations rolled in. I had held myself separate from others in an effort to protect myself. I was driven to be successful for the accolades and the safety that money could buy me. I judged fundamental religion as nonsense. I rejected corporations as beasts ready to gobble up innocent people on the road to making a profit. I despised George W. Bush as a war monger. I saw my parents as enemies. The ideas that had hovered around the edge of my consciousness for many months were beginning to take hold. I blushed in the dark with my embarrassment and shame. I didn't yet know what to do with this information. I was still assimilating it and trying to make meaning from it.

In that moment, the lights came back on and I was crying. Then, there were choking sobs that disturbed my breathing and made my head hurt. I lay down on my bed and cried. The deepest crying I had ever experienced. The cry of a lifetime is how I now view it.

Eventually, I cried myself to sleep.

Waking the next morning with the sun beaming through the curtains, every inch of my head hurt, and I had no reflective paper written for class that day. I headed to the shower, worried about all my unfinished work, and that I might not graduate.

Dear Reader,

As you read this section, reflect upon Principle #2 "Resolve Past Issues & Release Your Brain Power!" Sometimes the confluence of our present circumstances pierces a veil of something deep inside of us that screams for our attention. On the surface it might feel like an overreaction, but in reality, it's like lancing a wound so we can be healed. This is an indication that it's bigger and requires some attention. The break down and tears are required. Peace and freedom emerges when we shed the armor, that we've struggled so hard to keep in place, to protect us from our feelings—our internal guidance that leads us to the truth.

- *What unresolved issues from your past might be creating obstacles for you reaching your goals?*
- *What is preventing you from looking at these issues?*
- *What can you do to resolve these issues?*

CHAPTER 21

FINDING MY JUICE

THE SPRING DAYS were filled with new thunderstorms and streams of water rushed down the streets each afternoon. Our morning courses were much less interesting to me as I neared the end of the second semester—still worried about what lay ahead of me.

The computer lab was full every afternoon, and I found myself spending at least three days a week with my younger classmates in discussions about their possible career paths, while we worked on our theses. It was a little ironic that I didn't have a clue what I would do next with my own career. However, I was beginning to see that my twenty-five years of corporate work experience might be useful. I considered that maybe I had thrown the baby out with the bathwater on rejecting corporations. It was true that there were some greedy multinational corporations that exploited people and land. And there were plenty of corporations that did not do that and played to the triple bottom-line, measuring themselves on people, planet, and profit. That appealed to me.

That afternoon, I met with Adib from Lebanon, and we talked about his aspirations. He was an outgoing, warm, and quick-witted young man, only twenty-four years old. He wanted to go back to the Mideast and work for a corporation. He was open to being in any country except Israel. Just the month before, he had circulated a picture of the staged mass protest by Hezbollah in Lebanon. The picture showed his contemporaries with pro-Palestinian and anti-Israeli demonstrators.

I asked what he liked about corporations and he responded with, "I can make a lot of money and have job security. It is the quickest legal way to make money."

Wow. Maybe I had hugely overplayed my hatred-of-corporate hand.

On the bus the next morning, Alphonse sat next to me. I asked what he planned to do when he returned home. "Cindy, I will be bringing home the information and curriculum I learned at UPEACE." he proudly stated, adding that he planned to return to the Center for Conflict Management affiliated with the National University of Rwanda. He smiled with his big broad smile that melted my heart. He chose his dreams, and he chose his future. I admired him then and still do today.

When I was not working on my thesis, I scoured websites for non-profit leadership opportunities in San Diego. This seemed an easier search than doing the detailed research on whether or not a corporation was triple-bottom-line. I found an executive director (ED) opening in San Diego for the Tariq Khamisa Foundation (TKF). Tariq was killed while attending San Diego State University and delivering pizzas to earn spending money. On a home pizza delivery, fourteen-year-old gang-member, Tony Hicks shot and killed Tariq as his initiation into the gang.

Sadness and violence again.

Yet, Tariq's father, Azim did something different. He did his forgiveness work and forgave Tony. Then along with Tony's grandfather, Ples Felix, they formed TKF to teach non-violence, forgiveness, and anti-gang programs in primary and middle schools in San Diego. They were now looking to scale the programs.

I was so moved by their mission and the alignment with my recent peace and violence studies that I sent an email indicating my interest in applying for the position. I was so excited that I emailed Dana that night to call me. I couldn't possibly wait for our regularly scheduled call in the morning. I shared about the opportunity, and she pulled up the TKF website as we talked. She agreed that it was a match for my skills and was aligned with my new personal mission to peacefully contribute to others. She was ecstatic that I could possibly have a position lined up when I returned home for which I had a real passion and a commitment.

I requested letters of reference from several leaders in San Diego who knew of my skills and my character, and who also knew Azim Khamisa. They regarded him to be of the highest caliber, a leader for us all to emulate. I was getting more and more excited about this possibility. I wrote and rewrote my resume and cover letter several times. I shared it with Dana and my trusted University for Peace colleagues for review and edits. Within five days, I submitted my completed package to the chair of the board of the Tariq Khamisa Foundation. I was a bit nervous, and yet had a calm confidence that if this was my next step, I would be offered the position. I heard back from the acting executive director within two days, requesting a face-to-face interview. We found a workable date, one week later where I could fly home and not miss much coursework.

I met the four staff members for breakfast at Hob Nob Hill, a historical San Diego restaurant just about ten minutes from the airport. The interview was scheduled for 1.5 hours. I had just enough time to make my flight back to San Jose after breakfast. Two hours had flown as they spoke about their work to show young people a more satisfying way to resolve differences. They were deeply interested in hearing about the University for Peace and the Peace Army. Our time together was so fun for me. After hugs all the way around, I rushed to the airport for my flight back to Costa Rica.

As I dashed onto the airplane at the last possible minute, I sat down with a sigh and a good feeling that it had gone well. As I replayed the interview in my mind, I looked for areas that I could have responded better or answered more clearly. Nothing critical popped in.

They had said I would hear within a week about whether or not I was to be moved forward to the next interview with the chair of the board. I had done my part and was content with my preparation—and did my best to keep hope alive as I waited for a decision. That night back in my Ciudad Colon apartment, I sent a thank you letter to the four women that had interviewed me just that morning and shared my renewed excitement about the position. I also reached out to my colleagues and references to let them know the interview had gone well and thanked them for their support and efforts on my behalf. I promised to keep them in the loop and went back to my thesis and completing my coursework over the next week.

One week went by with no information. I just figured they were busy.

At the ten-day mark, I contacted the acting executive director, asking where they were in their hiring process. She indicated that it was now in the hands of the board chair, and he would be the next person to contact me. Having made several hires in my career, I knew the process well. Once she submitted her recommendation to the chair, the decision was out of her hands. He was the next step in the process and the final decision maker.

By day thirty after the interview, I knew that something must have happened when I did not hear anything from the chair. The posting had been pulled from the website, and I had sent two emails to the chair with no response. I sent out one last email to the acting executive director. She professionally described that the chair had decided to take over in the acting ED role and they would not be hiring a permanent ED, at this time.

I was so bummed that I left school right after class and went to the soda café in town to eat tacos with the Columbian owner—and sulk. I had two months until graduation, and I didn't have a new career in mind for my return to San Diego. I thought it was going to be easy to discover, and I would excitedly embark on my new career when I returned from Costa Rica. I began to wonder about my naïve thoughts. I wondered if my year of living off the grid in Costa Rica was really just an escape from my previously unbalanced career rather than going toward something that was healthier and integrated all parts of my life.

At this point, I had honed my meditation and spiritual practice skills to see that I was headed down the rabbit hole of anxiety and despair. I stopped, lit a candle, moved to my mediation cushion, and at the completion of the meditation, I created two mantras. "I surrender to the power and presence within." I finally knew that control wasn't always the best avenue to success. The second mantra was, "The Divine Spirit within me provides the right employment by 7/1/2005." Knowing that I could say these two mantras each day would stop my panic about my unfound new career and release it into the universe to solve.

Besides, I had my final course work that desperately needed my attention. I threw myself into my research and writing sections of my Peace Army thesis. My classmates were also focused on writing their theses. This meant fewer evening parties and dinner get-togethers. We were all holed up in our little apartments or the computer lab to get the theses written so we could graduate with our newly minted master's degrees in ten weeks.

I attended classes, wrote my thesis, and swam laps at the local pool. This was the fastest and easiest way to get exercise, since I had sprained my ankle. There did not seem to be time for much else. Yet, when my little Unity Church offered the 4T Class I signed up. It was advertised as a program in prosperity transformation and commitment to change. The four T's stood for tithe, time, talent, and treasure. The agreements to join the program were to tithe—an old school word for contribute, generally understood to be 10% of one's income.

Assisting in the Sunday morning services at the Unity Church met my time in service requirement. Check. I contributed my talent with my meaningful work at the Peace Army and my UPEACE work in the La Carpio neighborhood. Check. My treasure was to be 10% of my income, to the church during the seven weeks of the program. Not a check.

The tithing concept gave me pause. I had tithed for a three-year period of time as Board President at the Center for Spiritual Living church that I attended in San Diego. Tithing was a requirement for serving on the board. When I was honest with myself, I felt comfortable tithing because I reviewed the financials each month and knew the money was being used appropriately. This new situation felt different.

I generally gave money to charity and causes when friends and family asked for money to assist them in their humanitarian work. Again, honestly it was in support of my friends and family and their goals. I had committed myself to raising money for AIDS patient services, and in doing so had ridden my bicycle 560 miles from San Francisco to Los Angeles three different years and had raised over $25,000. Dana and I had also raised $22,000 and trekked in South Africa to fund an AIDS vaccine project. I was proud of our efforts to physically train and raise the money. These all seemed like good causes and made us feel like we had contributed to our world. But tithing to a church where I didn't see the books?

All of these thoughts went through my mind as I considered the 10% tithe requirement. I didn't even have an income to calculate the 10% against. In a conversation with the program leader, we settled on 10% on top of my current monthly living expenses budget of $650. I gulped and began contributing $16 per week for the seven weeks of the 4T program.

One of our first exercises was to create a vision board on an 8.5" by 11" sheet of paper that was a visual representation of my vision of the future—one that could be posted to remind me of my intention. I began with a meditation and then flipped through old magazines for nearly two hours cutting out various words and pictures that caught my attention. I carefully pasted my pictures and phrases onto my vision board and was crying as I completed the exercise.

I realized I could not go back to corporate work. I had completed that portion of my life. Inspiration and spirituality now eclipsed safety and security in my world. I didn't know how the vision board would come into reality, but I was clear that I was moving towards it. My vision board main topics were life without fear, ancient wisdom meets technology, and beyond the importance of success is spirituality, inspiration, and fun—lots of fun.

One of the most powerful exercises was to list the gifts I would express and give to the world. My natural gifts list was easy to populate: energetic, inspired, smart, funny, generous, authentic, leadership, and an ability to see the best in people. My learned gifts also flowed: project management, organizational change, team building, conflict resolution, facilitator, trainer, and educator.

Now we are getting somewhere. I could use this information as criteria to compare possible career paths against. This is going to be worth the $112 tithe.

On the edge of my mind, I noted that I could also choose to give out of generosity—and not look to what I would gain from the experience. This generous approach of giving my gifts and trusting that financial reward would follow was barely beginning to poke through my consciousness. I didn't yet know this would be the cornerstone of my new career approach in management consulting.

Dear Reader,

*Principle #3 states "Discover What Juices You—and Pursue It."
Getting clarity on what juiced me was the first step. I didn't
really know how I was going to get where I was going, but I
knew I would. The how shows up—Principle #6, "Move to
Action!" We often want to wait until we know every step before
we move, and that creates paralysis. Like many great masters,
such as Lao Tzu and Martin Luther King, Jr., have said, the
journey always begins with the first step. And it's important to
have passion driving our direction.*

- *What excites you so much that you would pursue it even
  without compensation?*
- *What is stopping you from following your passion?*
- *What is the one next right move you can take toward your
  dream?*

CHAPTER 22

ENLIGHTENMENT IN LA CARPIO

EVEN A PEACEFUL NATION such as Costa Rico has its danger zones, where a pocket of poverty is fertile for unrest, violence, and crime. San Jose had La Carpio.

La Carpio was the poorest neighborhood in Costa Rica and had earned a reputation among the locals as a violent area. The slum was an impoverished community and home to nearly 20,000 people, half Nicaraguan immigrants and half Costa Rican nationals. It was located about five miles northwest of Costa Rica's capital, San Jose, and shamelessly visible from two major east-west highways that ran from San Jose.

As part of our UPEACE course work, we were to conduct action projects. Abelardo chose La Carpio for our project, and one sunny afternoon, the University for Peace bus took us to the La Carpio neighborhood for a tour in preparation of our project. It turns out that Abelardo lived nearer La Carpio than UPEACE, so he followed the bus in his car so he could head home after the afternoon tour.

Our class was welcomed by a leader of an NGO, and he immediately instructed us to be careful as we stepped off the bus in a downwardly sloping field that was filled with trash. I squinted as I looked directly into the bright sunlight of the La Carpio barrio that I had only seen from the highway. There were four mounds of trash about 25 feet high, 100 feet to our left. Eight boys and a couple of girls were running amidst the trash piles playing soccer. As I followed the direction of their running and the half-deflated soccer ball, I saw their creativity in action. Rusted metal frames from a machine of some sort served as their two goals. The kids were dressed in torn shorts and t-shirts, wore no shoes, and had mud and dirt in their hair and on their skin. I imagined they did not shower or bathe regularly. That little nuisance did not stop them from playing their little hearts out.

They were yelling to each other for the ball as they kicked it and laughed. They stopped their game when they realized we were on the hill watching them and all wildly waved their welcome to the neighborhood. One little girl's bright smile sent a knife into my heart. Her free spirit dancing on the field reminded me much of my own as a child. I sensed she found her freedom running after the ball.

I smiled with joy and felt tears of sadness at the same time.

My fellow classmates and I descended the steep red dirt hillside to the makeshift stairs, which led us to a wooden plank that crossed the narrow flowing stream down the center of La Carpio. Houses were clinging to both sides of the embankment. We visited ten different homes, all with the same configuration. The houses were made with haphazardly sized wood, tin siding, and random roofing materials nailed to the wood that formed a 12-by-12 square foot house with two dirt floor rooms. One room was set aside for cooking and eating, and one for sleeping the entire family, regardless of their numbers and gender. There was no visible plumbing or electricity in this area near the stream. As we toured the village, we crossed over the little stream several times. I noticed the open sewage floating by and the offending smell assaulted my senses. The host in each home was generally an older woman. She was maybe a mother or grandmother, but clearly the one that stayed at the home during the day.

As we walked up the dirt road to the top of the hillside, there was a pot-holed asphalt road that met up with the dirt road. I saw cinder block homes now. They were of similar construction to the majority of homes in Costa Rica. Yet, these homes were in a state of disrepair with crumbling concrete, peeling paint, and exposed rebar.

We aimed toward several buildings surrounded by a 10-foot tall fence and an armed guard posted at the gate. It looked prison-like and I was surprised when it was the primary school that we would next visit. After the guard unlocked the gate and welcomed us, we walked through the playground with hundreds of kids running around on recess. We poked our heads into classrooms and were welcomed by several teachers and young students. Many, it seemed, were primed for a mini-presentation for their UPEACE visitors.

With the language barrier, I caught most of what was said, but said very little in my elementary Spanish that was understood by teachers or students. As we finished up the day in the cafeteria with little sugar cookies and sugar-laden red punch, it was time to board the UPEACE bus back to the school. I made what I expected to be a brief stop at the restroom, but when I emerged to board the bus, the parking lot was almost empty. There was no bus to be seen. Somehow the bus departed without a head count or a check on anyone that was missing. This was not unusual in Costa Rica, but still presented a dilemma for me about how to get back to Ciudad Colon.

I was relieved to see Abelardo's car still in the parking lot. My relief, it turned out, was premature. Whatever misgivings I had about Abelardo were soon proven.

I found Abelardo and a teacher talking; I asked how to get a taxi back to Ciudad Colon. I stood with my laptop and files in a computer bag draped over my shoulder as Abelardo translated my English request to the teacher in Spanish. After she replied to Abelardo with her head shaking back and forth, I realized this would not be as easy as I imagined.

Abelardo held his hands together as if they were heavy to explain to me in his perfect Buddhist way that "unfortunately taxi drivers refused to serve La Carpio because of the crime, gangs, and general violence."

Oh, that is just great.

And as usual, Abelardo was deferentially leaning his large frame towards me with an odd smile and kind eyes that were not interested at all in solving my problem. Instead, it was the usual, uni-directional reporting of information.

Breathe. Breathe.

I hoped the teacher was a problem solver as I asked Abelardo to ask her if there was a bus that went to Ciudad Colon from La Carpio. He once again dutifully translated, and she once again shook her head as they conversed. My anxiety was increasing as I noticed the sun going down behind the westward mountains of Costa Rica.

Abelardo again explained in his gentle giant, non-helpful, smiling kind of way that there were no buses for the same reason. Nobody came to La Carpio unless you lived here, worked here, or were invited here. I thought of the lyrics to "Hotel California" by the Eagles: "You can check out anytime you like, but you can never leave."

Fabulous. I am in a crime-ridden neighborhood that taxi drivers refuse to serve, the city refuses to offer bus service to, and I am standing in a dirt parking lot with armed guards with Mr. 'I can't solve any problem' Abelardo.

I looked at Abelardo, "Ask her what idea might she have for me to get back to Ciudad Colon?"

Again, Abelardo translated and she said, in Spanish that I understood, "Why don't you drive her home, Abelardo?"

I figured he could not refuse with her standing right there. He tightly smiled, struggling to maintain his Buddha face with this suggestion dangling between us. He said, "Yes, I can do that."

Jumping on the opportunity before he came up with a reason to change his mind, I thanked them both and quickly headed towards Abelardo's car with my computer bag slung over my shoulder.

As the guard opened the gate to let Abelardo's car escape the school grounds, the sun was setting, and it was now twilight—that time of day that is not yet night and beautifully shadowed with grays and boogie men.

We drove along in silence for about a mile before he said, "I will let you off around this next curve and you can walk about two kilometers to the bus stop. The bus goes directly to Ciudad Colon."

He had lost all Buddha nature and was being very matter of fact.

Then I was afraid. I had never trusted him, but the weird change of demeanor caught me completely off guard. I was used to the bumbling professor with the angelic Buddha peaceful smile that could not dialogue. Irritating as it was, it had become a familiar demeanor after nine months together. He pulled to the edge of the road and a dirt pathway to let me off.

"Which direction is the bus stop?" I asked, trying to remain calm. I had never been in this part of the city and did not own a cell phone, let alone a GPS.

"Down about two kilometers on this path, around the bend to the right will be the bus stop to Ciudad Colon," he curtly replied.

His change in demeanor had freaked me out. I stepped out of the car onto the dirt pathway. The cars on the two-lane road were zooming past with their lights on and I realized just how dark it was. I didn't see any good way to cross the road to the other side so I cautiously continued walking on the right-hand side of the road. There were overgrown bushes on the outer side of the path on both sides of the road and about every three minutes somebody walked toward me from the opposite direction on the path.

My fear of being in the dark, alone, lost, and my location unknown to anyone was amplified. I remembered the reason that taxis and buses didn't come here. I remembered the guide in La Carpio talking about the level of violence. He talked about rapes, murders, drug activity, and generally bad actors running around La Carpio at will. I wondered if the police even came to the area or if they were also afraid and stayed away.

I kept looking over my shoulder to be aware of my surroundings, as I had learned in self-defense class ten years earlier. I went through all my possible moves I could make to free myself, if somebody came from behind me, from the bushes beside me, or came towards me. I switched my computer bag to my left shoulder to slow down a robber that could jump from the bushes from my right and just grab my computer off my right shoulder. Anything to make it hard or slow down a would-be robber.

Thinking was slowing me down, and my conjecture and bad scenario musings had made sweat drip down my back and my heart quicken. I picked up my pace and told myself to stop thinking so much. As I finished the curve to the right, I came on an intersection with a traffic signal. I stopped in my tracks. To the right were three men talking and laughing with each other. As I pondered my next move, I looked at the bright lights to the left.

It was the United States Embassy with a giant American flag and three crisp marines in their dress uniforms with rifles standing at the entrance.

I ran across the intersection and nervously cried with joy, as relief washed over my body and fear dissipated. The marines were understandably cautious as I ran up the stairs towards them. "Stop right there," one of them said. "Who are you and what business do you have here?"

I hurriedly told them who I was, showed a copy of my U.S. Passport and explained how I found myself walking alone with my computer bag, a couple of miles from La Carpio.

They were about twenty-five years old, about the same age as the other students at UPEACE. I don't think my story of being a mature student of forty-six years old at the University for Peace seemed plausible. After answering several more questions, their skepticism turned to empathy, and they seemed eager to help me get back to Ciudad Colon. One young marine smiled, and after clearing it with somebody inside the embassy on his walkie-talkie, said he would walk me to the bus stop. I wanted to hug these young men, but I was sure that would break protocol. Instead, I shook their hands and thanked them for their kindness.

The bus stop was in fact where I had earlier seen the other guys standing on the corner. I thanked my protector, as the bus arrived and I boarded for my thirty-minute ride to Ciudad Colon, choosing a seat next to an older woman. As I looked out the window into complete darkness, I reflected on my fearful experience. On the surface, I was pissed at the UPEACE bus driver for leaving me in the first place. Then I was pissed at Abelardo for being such a weirdo and dropping me in the middle of nowhere.

Deeper than all of that, I was surprised at my immediate relief at the sight of the American flag and the U.S. Marines. My fear immediately disappeared. Was it that being an American had currency, even in Costa Rica? I think it was knowing that they would help me and protect me because I was an American citizen.

I thought of my harsh critique of the U.S. showing military might. I saw flaws in my previous simplistic thinking about the military. In fact, it is not the military that is the issue. These young men and women are well trained to serve. It is actually the politics and expert judgment of when to use might and power that was the question for me. So, I pondered that maybe the presence of might and power were all that was needed in most situations, reserving the judicious use of power for the bad actors who were perpetuating crimes and human rights violations.

Maybe power and might should not ever come from fear or anger. That was more like rage or revenge—much like my father's behavior, and even my own when I wielded the knife, aiming to use it against him if he acted out of line those many years ago in my childhood living room.

Is it possible that our fears drive our need to overpower others? What if we could see our fears, not act on them, and choose another way to act or respond?

I wondered what my father feared as he used his power over all of us. And on my bus ride back to Cuidad Colon, I contemplated whether or not one could be powerful and not violent.

Dear Reader,

When we can understand what fear can drive us to, we can have compassion and resolve how to have "power with" rather than "power over." It's so easy to have an opinion without having facts and without understanding another viewpoint that is so shortsighted. It sets up "us versus them" or "me versus you." I could not have been more shocked at myself, at my excitement, and my relief to see the U.S. Embassy and see young marines with guns. I had very strong opinions about my country and what was wrong at that time. Yet when I was fearful, I was happy to see the marines. There is a whole bunch of privilege that came with that. My circumstances changed immediately because I am a U.S. citizen and the privilege that comes with that. I realized I had been forming judgments based on my own "narrow" viewpoints and getting my information on 24-hour news bites.

- *Where are you forming judgments about situations without having all the information?*
- *Where are you creating "us versus them" stories?*
- *Where might learning more about situations actually lead you to greater understanding?*

CHAPTER 23

EXPLORING POWER WITH

As I walked to the bus stop the next morning, my experience in La Carpio the previous night had shaken something loose in my belief system. *What if there was a way to change my thinking from simplistic views of military as "power over" to a view of "power with"?* An idea began to form as I approached the bus stop and my classmates.

After our pleasantries, I used the bus ride as an experiment to test out my nuanced thinking about the military with a few choice colleagues. I first asked Patrick, "How do you see the United States in general and the U.S. military specifically?"

"I see the United States with freedoms that I wish every country would have. But I see the U.S. military as occupiers that interfere too often in other country's sovereignty," he elegantly expressed. He then went on a rant about President Bush and his invasion of Iraq. I acknowledged his view and hurriedly helped him to complete that thought before I asked the next question.

"Do you have any positive views of the U.S. military?" I genuinely asked.

"Sometimes they help people, like with the tsunami," he added as he thought a little deeper. "But not really."

I next sat next to Muzy, from Uzbekistan, and asked him the same questions. He was much more versed in the politics of the U.S. and said,

"I believe the U.S. has freedoms that the former Soviet Union didn't give to its people. That, I believe, is good. But George Bush is crazy. He invades countries even when he doesn't have to. All for U.S. oil interests."

He went on to explain, "U.S. power works fine when you are an ally of the U.S., but you don't ever want to be an enemy because they can declare war, invade your country and bomb you to hell, anytime they wish. They do this with their enemies, except for Russia and China," he shared.

I now had an Eastern European and African view. I wanted a U.S. view. I moved to sit next to Tory, my friend from Wyoming. "Tell me how you think of the U.S. foreign policies in general and the U.S. military specifically," I asked her.

"George Bush and Dick Cheney are neo-cons. Iraq is the same thing the U.S. did in Vietnam. American interests above everything else. Vietnam was a proxy war with the Soviets and Iraq is all about America's dependence on oil. Always American interests and at the detriment of the country, their people, and their way of life. It is disrespectful, in my opinion," she shared.

I looked out the bus window, as we passed coffee farms with poor migrant workers tending the coffee bushes along the hillsides—coffee beans that might wind up in my neighborhood Starbucks in San Diego.

Then, several ideas crashed together at once. The U.S. military provided safety and security for the U.S. and many other nations globally. There was an important role to play against bad actors, for sure. Also, the U.S. government quite possibly had a public relations problem when it came to the military. Having worked in the military industrial complex, I knew that the Department of Defense (DOD) spent tremendous funds on Research and Development (R&D). I also knew that my General Dynamic colleagues were smart engineers, scientists, mathematicians, and business people creating technology for the military—and shared many of the same values about health and well-being for their families, freedom, and access to education. These were indeed the same values that my UPEACE classmates yearned for.

How could that concept be conveyed and a more sophisticated view be brought forward?

I had a brand-new idea for my class project.

I completed writing my paper on "New Uses for United States Department of Defense Funds" and was figuring out how to create a presentation that enrolled my classmates in a completely different viewpoint about the U.S. military. It would be something more aligned with my new progressive viewpoint of safety and security, but not at the expense of power over people.

In my research, I found two predominate causes of conflict and war in the twenty-first century. The first was a perceived need to fight to preserve cultural values and identity. Basic human needs theory states that certain ontological and genetic needs of safety and security, when challenged by an evolution of socialization that does not include their voice or their needs, will lead to frustrations, anti-social behaviors, and even violence.

The second large cause of conflict and war in the twenty-first century was over control and access to natural resources. As an example, since 1950, the renewal supply of fresh water per person has fallen 58% as world population swelled from 2.5 billion to 6.5 billion people in 2005. The U.S. dependence on oil, sourced from the Middle East, was another example of a natural resource need.

I contemplated what could be done to avoid war over identity or cultural differences and the tug-of-war over natural resources. Many argued in my research that military coercion and military might was not the answer. My thinking took me to consider what if the military could preserve general operating funds, the safety and security aspect of spending, and divert some R&D spending and repurpose technology intended for the next best weapon to social and environmental solutions.

In 2004, DOD spending was nearly $400 billion, half of all military expenditures in the world. The spend trend was on the rise after the "War on Terror" was declared after the 9/11 attacks on the World Trade Center in New York. Of that budget, 17% of the budget was for Research and Development.

This was not a new idea I discovered. In the 1990s, at the conclusion of the Cold War, the DOD introduced a Domestic Technology Transfer (T2) Program and Dual Use Program as a way to use the DOD technology for commercial purposes. The T2 program directive stated that, "Domestic T2 activities are integral elements of DOD pursuit of the DOD national security mission and to concurrently improve the economic, social and environmental well-being of U.S. citizens."

The precedent was already set! It was now a matter of overcoming small thinking and prioritizing spending for larger reasons that needed to be revealed through my presentation to my classmates.

There were examples in the literature of several environmentally useful technologies. Desalination technology used on U.S. Navy ships could be used to convert seawater to safe drinking water in those regions with clean water shortages. Satellite technology originally developed for surveillance could be used for early warning systems in tracking hurricanes, tornados, monsoons, tsunamis, and volcano eruptions.

Examples of socially useful technologies included information technology that could be used to perform remote surgery in third world countries by skilled surgeons thousands of miles away guiding the hands of local health care professionals. Another was using miniaturized cameras in pill form to view the body from the inside without invasive surgery, potentially revolutionizing worldwide healthcare.

I was so excited at the possibilities that I no longer needed to hold the U.S. military at arm's length in my mind. I could embrace it for the security aspects it did so well and envision a time of great national and global leadership, with the positive global impacts created by using DOD technology for social, environmental and economic solutions. Interestingly, these expenditures could also contribute to more safety and security globally—fitting into the overall U.S. military mission.

My presentation was set up for the class members to role-play people from the DOD that were making recommendations on prioritizing U.S. military spending. They were to consider their priority to provide for the safety and security of U.S. citizens and to look at the alleged controversy between the Pentagon and those that believe the U.S. spends too much on its military, namely the peaceniks and the environmentalists. By presenting facts to the group and recognizing their other role as parents and grandparents, perhaps they could come up with a spending plan that satisfied more than one set of needs.

The class first needed to be educated on the facts and trends in spending. Facts were presented about U.S. military spending over the previous fifty years. Since WWII, funding had generally trended downward after a military war, during years of peace. Much of the U.S. spending after WWII was diverted to building U.S. infrastructure, bridges, and the interstate system. Foreign spending was focused on the Marshall Plan and rebuilding Europe and Japan.

However, this trend changed in the Reagan years with a U.S. weaponry build up during the Cold War. After the Berlin Wall fell and the USSR was dissolved, the U.S. again decreased its spending and diverted re-purposed military technology from primary uses of weaponry and surveillance to social, environmental, and economic uses.

I could see the class was stunned to hear these facts. As I imagined,

Patrick was the first to ask, "Why then did the U.S. invade Iraq, if the dual use of military technology was so benevolent?"

I turned to the class, "Any ideas?" This turned out to be a mistake as there was a major pile-on about George Bush's foreign policy and narrow views of the world. I reminded my peers of their DOD member roles and asked what the average global citizen may not understand about the role of the DOD. The group eventually declared that global citizens didn't recognize the good things the military does in humanitarian crises. Then, Muzy offered, "Small rebel incursions should not be left to the U.S. to unilaterally resolve but should be left to the U.N. to resolve. The U.N. Peacekeepers could ask for U.S. military assistance, if needed."

Then I asked, "Are there some environmental and social solutions that lead to more safety and security?"

This began a very lively debate about the need for clean water and the U.S. dependence on oil. Suddenly, we were on the topics that I had hoped to have them discussing—namely, how to sustain a strong and operational military for protection, safety, and security *and* invest in more complex thinking around solving for the root causes of war and violence by investing in programs that created increased global economic viability, better use of limited natural resources, and more independent and sustainable nations.

Riding home on the bus that afternoon, I reveled in the morning discussion and the out-of-the-box solutions that stretched the mind to imagine. This got my mind pointed at non-traditional thinking in traditional systems. This is what excited me—and what led me to a solution and my career decision.

Viewing myself as a better speaker than writer, each writing activity up until that point was full of effort and angst, including my thesis. I also struggled that my ideas would go no further than my professors' desks. Since Eliana and Amr were now my thesis advisors, I didn't have to follow the purely academic and, in my mind, nonsensical direction of Abelardo. The Peace Army thesis would be put into action and was sure to scale to create profound outcomes in Costa Rica. The bad news was that I still had to write this paper to finish my master's program.

One afternoon, I had scheduled six hours to work on my thesis and I could not focus. My mind kept wandering to consider all the possibilities of my new career. I closed the thesis file on my laptop and found my stash of yellow stickies and my black pen. On each sticky, I wrote one question: *What had I learned about myself this past year? What did I like? What were my strengths that brought me energy? What didn't I like and where was my energy drained?* I began furiously writing my thoughts as they came forward. I just wrote until I didn't have anything else to add. I then organized the stickies into affinity groups and began to get clarity about what I really wanted to do in my career—and what I didn't want to do.

I liked working with people and not computer systems. I enjoyed learning about people, cultures, and beliefs. I wanted to contribute to people in some way to improve their plight. Or if they were not in dire circumstances, to assist in some way to achieve the best self they could imagine. The work needed to involve dialogue and deep listening, listening for the soul's joy, not meaningless exchanges of pleasantries. The work also must engage the higher purposes in life. The mind-body-spirit connection was vital for me to engage with on a daily basis. If these values were appreciated in the workplace, all the better.

International work was intriguing, but I did not want to do humanitarian work on the ground for an extended period of time. My emotions could not handle it. *Maybe a business emphasis to create economic development and personal economic viability?* Microcredit was beginning to catch on, and Mohammed Yunnus and Grameen Bank had loaned a total of $4.7 billion USD to women in $20-$50 loans over twenty years in Bangladesh. That was something I could really get involved with. I could work at a microcredit bank, on the ground in a developing country. This would require a mix of business skills and communication/dialogue skills. *Perfect!* With that settled, for the moment, I went back to writing my thesis and made significant writing progress that afternoon.

Eight o'clock on the dot, Dana phoned the next morning. I didn't even ask about her previous day before I was blurting out that I had found my life's work! I quickly explained, "Microcredit was an amazing concept to provide micro-loans of $20-50 to women in developing countries to purchase their goods or supplies to create their businesses. Examples were buying a chicken to sell eggs, or buying a cart to push through town loaded with her prepared food like tamales, tacos, burritos. I know a ton more examples, when we have more time to talk about it."

Dana calmly said, "I think that is a perfect match for your skills and your interests."

"There is a microcredit annual conference in November in Halifax, Nova Scotia, Canada. Do you want to go with me?"

"Let's do it. It would be fun to learn together. We haven't been to Nova Scotia," she answered.

I was so happy to feel like I had a direction and that Dana supported me in that direction.

She added, "As long as you do your international work from San Diego."

I froze. I assumed I would be doing international work abroad, not from San Diego.

"What do you mean?" I asked. "How would I do that?"

"The International Rescue Committee (IRC) and several other international non-profits are in San Diego. I would not be surprised if there are microcredit programs in the immigrant communities of San Diego," she explained to me.

"Well, I guess I had always thought that you would retire, and I was going to work abroad," I sheepishly said.

"I am not ready to retire or quit yet. I still have five more years. Besides, you have been gone almost a year and you need to stay home for a while. I am not saying you can't travel abroad, but we need to agree on the timeframes. Maybe a month abroad and a month home or two weeks gone and two weeks home. I need you to be home!" she appealed.

In a split second, I fell from the stars back to earth and could not see how I was going to do international work at all. Yet, I knew exactly what she was talking about. I had been gone almost a year and had the luxury of no financial obligations and no timeframes. I could wander about in my mind on intellectually stimulating topics or wander around Costa Rica on adventures anytime I wished. It was time for me to come home and stay home for a while.

"You are right," I said glumly.

"I am not saying that you can't do international work. I am just saying I need you to be with me. I've missed you terribly and want to see you every day," she shared from her heart.

After our call, I reflected that I had always figured everything out by myself. I was now counting on my Spirit to guide me. But it was still all me. I didn't count on or trust other people. Not even Dana.

Dear Reader,

When we are embracing the theory of "power with," and challenge the status quo, we often discover resources that allow us to go in a new direction. Conversations are not focused on the "me"; it shifts to "we" and empowers others to share their ideas and solutions. We shift from it's not my problem to solve to it's in our power to solve. It empowers individuals who aren't usually given voice (Principle #5). So, consider the following:

- *What in you has to change/shift to move from "my" problem to "our" problem?*
- *What are the risks that you take in doing so?*
- *What are your thoughts about sharing power?*
- *What skills do you need to learn to shift the burden of responsibility?*

CHAPTER 24

OPENING THE DOOR TO FORGIVENESS

THE FIRST YEAR OF cycle training for the California AIDS ride was in 1998. Dana and I had decided to ride our bikes 560 miles from San Francisco to Los Angeles to raise money for AIDS Services in both California cities. Several of our male gay friends had died terrible deaths from AIDS, and this fundraiser felt like a small way we could positively contribute to the pandemic.

Bicycle training ramped up to about seventy-five miles per week through the spring of 1998. Every six weeks or so I was also visiting my parents for a long weekend in Tennessee since my dad had been diagnosed with non-small cell lung cancer in 1997. My sister, Deb, was traveling from Texas to visit at opposite times from me to help our parents. My mom was his primary caregiver, and, through her gallant efforts, she was able to keep his meds straight and take him to his doctors' appointments while performing all his daily care. She later told me that the first and forty-second year, their last, were the happiest of their marriage.

In the meantime, my dad was tired all the time, and carried around a portable oxygen tank so he could still putter in the yard and his garden. The tumor in his lung was inoperable, and when they shrank it with radiation about five months after he was diagnosed, it gave him easier breathing and one additional year of life. We didn't know when he would pass, but my mom, sister, and I all needed to do all we could in those final months of his life to make him comfortable. He still had vestiges of anger when he would be frustrated with his situation, which was understandable. But I also still had the "young Dad" memories. The man that physically, verbally, psychologically, and emotionally abused us.

I worked hard during those months to get myself back to the excited young child that adored my dad. I set that state of mind as a personal goal. I wanted to give him true forgiveness and release him into his next time and place in the cosmos. I did know that forgiveness of him was actually to release me from my own self-imposed suffering at this point. The actions were twenty-five years earlier, and he could not hurt me now. But on the plane rides back to San Diego after a weekend with Dad and Mom, I found that I was just doing my daughterly obligatory trips. After all my efforts and therapy, I had not really forgiven him.

On Friday, May 29, my phone rang at 4:30 a.m. I jumped up out of a dead sleep and answered it. My sister said, "Cin, Dad wants to talk to you."

In a clear voice, with no wheezing or coughing voice, I heard my dad say, "Good morning, Doll. I hear you are off to your bike race today," with the vocal rise at the end of a sentence that sounded more like a question.

"Yes, today, we are off to San Francisco to stay overnight. Tomorrow, we will attend the expo and re-unite with our bikes that were shipped ahead. Then on Sunday morning at 7:00 a.m., we take off for seven days of riding," I explained, like he really wanted to hear it.

"It sounds like fun," he says.

My world was upside down. If I didn't know my dad's voice, I would not have said this was him. He was dying of lung cancer, never called me, and certainly hadn't asked me about myself for decades. *What was going on?*

"I just wanted to call and tell you that I love you, and I am so sorry I hurt you. I know I have told you before. But I want to make sure you have forgiven me for everything that I did," he very deliberatively shared.

I was crying too much to really hear his entire statement. This was his final confession, and he wanted to make things right with me before he died. I said, "I know Dad, I love you, too. Should I come back there, Dad?"

"No. I want you to do your ride and pour it on and win that race, Doll," he said as his voice trailed off.

Deb came back on the phone line to hear my muffled crying. "Are you ok, Cin?" she sweetly asked.

"I guess I am. What is happening?" I asked her. "Is he dying right now?"

"He has asked to speak with everyone he has harmed. He already talked to Mom, then me—and now you. We are lining up his mom, brothers and sisters to visit for about ten minutes each so he can complete his relationship with each person," she explained.

"Wow. That is amazing. Do you want me to come back, Deb?" I asked.

"You don't need to, Cin. Like we talked before, you have trained for a whole year for this ride. You should go on it. Besides, I heard Dad say you didn't need to come back. He is complete and who knows when he will pass, Cin. Go do your ride and call when you get back, and we will let you know what is going on," she kindly expressed. She had this handled.

I was torn listening to her. I didn't want her to feel obligated to do all the work on our behalf. Yet, I was thrilled that nobody was guilt-tripping me about coming back. My mom and I had talked when I visited on Mother's Day, a couple weeks earlier. "I'm going to go on my ride, even if that is the time that Dad chooses to pass on," I explained. "I needed to put myself first. I've put myself last for too long." This was one place I had decided to not take one for the team.

All this came flooding back into my mind while still on the phone with Deb. I was quite clear the month before; yet now, I wasn't as confident in my decision. In a split second, I decided, "I am going to do my ride, and I will call you next Saturday when I return. Thanks for taking care of things, Deb. I love you," I said through my tears.

"I love you, too," she said as she hung up.

Lying back down, I was wracked with sobs. He was such a brute all my life, and today he sounded like a normal person. Clear, direct, and with unabashed love and with no crazy anger. *Why could he not have been that man all his life?* Such a kind and gentle soul was covered up with low self-esteem and anger affecting all in his path. I said a simple prayer to let him live until I was back from my ride, and I could go back to help my mom and sister with the final arrangements.

This was not meant to be. He died the Wednesday of my ride. I found out on Saturday right after I crossed the finish line in Los Angeles.

As I understood the details on the phone, I realized that he had died the day I rode through Paso Robles and saw a farmer wave from his tractor. It was also the day that I went into the little mission and lit a candle for his soul.

Riding on the bus that morning in Costa Rica, I thought about how I did not count on anyone, not even Dana. After years of therapy, I knew that my independence and lack of trust came from a deep place in my childhood years. I could not count on my parents to protect me and knew that I needed to take care of myself—*and* my sisters.

Understanding more about the source of violence and watching my friend Alphonse model compassion and forgiveness after genocide, I decided that I needed to finish my forgiveness work of my parents to free myself from my self-imposed exile. I focused on forgiveness rituals and even set up an empty chair for my dad to sit in so I could freely talk to him. I wanted to express my disappointment about how I was treated and also to express my deep love for him. Then I talked to the empty chair that I imagined was my mom. While I could talk to her in person when she came to my graduation next month, I thought I should do some pre-work. During the process, I realized that I just wanted to know why she didn't protect me against Dad. She knew he was violent and beating all of us. "Why didn't you take us away?" I asked with tears flowing down my cheeks.

Next, I wanted to apologize to both my sisters. Deb was three years younger than me and lived in Texas. I decided I could talk to her when I went to her daughter's high school graduation the following week. Of course, my baby sister, Pam, was not available to speak with, now long dead, having died in a car accident at twenty-one, leaving behind her toddler daughter, Tiffany.

Imagining Pam in the empty chair, I said, "I'm sorry, Pam, for not keeping you safe while we were growing up." I heard in a feeling, rather than a voice, a very strong sense of her. She said, "You were great. The best big sister anyone could ever have. You loved us, took care of us, and I always knew everything would be okay, because you were there. No matter what!"

I was stunned. I didn't know she felt this way. Since she didn't need to forgive me, I knew I really needed to forgive myself. That was part of what Dad was doing with his deathbed confession and request for forgiveness. He was forgiving himself. It all made so much more sense to me.

I needed to forgive myself for not protecting my sisters. For not allowing myself to count on Dana. For not trusting others, for no longer liking my chosen career. For not knowing what my next career was. For blaming multinational corporations, religions, the military, for my misery. For not being perfect. For making mistakes. For not being generous.

After I wrote all these items of self-forgiveness on pieces of paper, I burned them in a sacred ritual that night. I lit candles, burned incense, and chanted mantras, touching my soul at a deep level, a level that could now be built upon for the remainder of my years on this planet. I felt light and free as I fell asleep that night. Forgiving my parents and myself left me lighter.

I now knew that all of humanity is connected on this life journey. Forgiveness did not mean accepting bad and violent behavior. It meant using our best efforts to manage our own lives and make the necessary changes to curb this behavior in the future. We also needed to act as survivors and not victims to break the cycle of violence in families, communities, businesses, and between nations.

Azim Khamisa forgave Tony, the young gang member, who shot and killed his son. Azim was the role model. He focused on his own forgiveness work, and he evolved to his own personal place of peace and created a program to end child-on-child violence.

Alphonse, from Rwanda, the little country in the Great Lakes region of Africa, touched my soul with his courage and focus on his family. Generously sharing his story allowed us to learn from the genocide atrocity and watch how he moved forward in his life.

By forgiving my dad—a man tortured by his own past and lack of confidence and esteem—I released the anger and moved to the place that Rumi describes as, "Out beyond the place of wrong-doing and right-doing there is a place. I will meet you there."

When I saw that opening, I realized there were many to forgive to soften my heart: my president for bad decisions that took us into two wars, and my company leaders for not always leading in the most effective ways. Abelardo for not being the example of a university professor that I wanted him to be.

In that moment, I decided to let go of needing to know what my new career would be. I knew and had proven to myself that I had gifts and talents to give the world. I decided I would be generous with them and trust that the money and the "new career" would follow. Perhaps it would be opposite of what I considered. Perhaps I would engage in a business career with peace skills rather than international peace work with business skills.

Dear Reader,

In The Four Sacred Gifts: Indigenous Wisdom for Modern Times, *Anita L. Sanchez, writes,*

"Forgiveness is a life-affirming, conscious act of power, not weakness, because the forgiver holds and uses this power to free and heal all those involved, both victim and perpetrator, so both can become whole human beings again." A person who is imprisoned by lack of forgiveness is only punishing themselves.

- *How can you free yourself from a self-imposed exile through forgiveness?*
- *Who can you forgive for any wrong doing?*
- *What do you need to forgive yourself for?*

CHAPTER 25

NOT AN END, BUT A BEGINNING

———————————

RECEIVING ANOTHER DEGREE was not nearly as important to me as the entirely new way of viewing my life. I still could not believe my good fortune for the opportunity to quit a corporate job that was literally killing me and attend the University for Peace that attracted world leaders in peace and amazing human beings from around the globe. Waves of gratitude engulfed me as we walked into the dressing area to don our graduation caps and gowns.

Camera flashes were going off all around the room as everyone was taking photos of classmates and now lifelong friends. Promises to not forget each other were being made in small huddles and smiles were everywhere.

Alphonse walked up to me and said, "Cindy, I will never forget you. I want you to visit me in Rwanda. I want you to meet my wife and sons."

"You better mean it," I said. "Dana and I travel a lot, and we may just be on your doorstep one day."

He grinned that big smile that touched my heart each time we talked. "I do mean it!" He emphatically announced.

I pulled him out of the lineup and brought him over to meet my mom. "Bobbie, this is Alphonse, from Rwanda. He and I have become good buddies during this year." I wanted her to know the man who had become so treasured in my life.

A little while later, as I proudly walked in the procession surrounded by my global friends, I sneaked a peak, and she was beaming and taking photos. *She is just so proud of me.* She had not attended my undergrad or grad school graduation ceremonies back in the eighties. I sensed a wrong being righted that day.

Dana, the seasoned photographer, was taking pictures like a true professional, capturing the scene of smiles, waves, and proud family, friends, and administrators in the audience. Her own mom was present as well for the festivities. I was surrounded by the loving women in my life as I took the stage to receive my diploma.

"Cynthia Lynn Henson," Dr. Amr Abdallah announced.

I hugged Amr and thanked him for contributing so freely to me this year. Then Abelardo was next in the line to shake my hand. I took his hand and looked up into his eyes and said, "Thank you for your work this year." I acknowledge that he was doing his best in the world, effective or not.

After the ceremony, it was time to say some farewells.

I walked up the verdant driveway lined with ginger bushes and bougainvilla to visit the Peace Army headquarters one last time. I entered the office to see Rita Marie hunched over her computer energetically typing with her intense stare focused on the computer screen. She didn't see me, but rather felt me walk into the office and jumped up with a smile and a hug for me.

"I am going home tomorrow," I shared as I sat down in a chair opposite her desk.

As she dropped back into her chair, she overflowed with love and appreciation. "Thank you so much for all you have done for the Peace Army this past year. I enjoyed your good ideas and your work towards improving the program. I really look forward to reading your Peace Army thesis," she said.

"I plan to finish the thesis in two weeks and will send to you for input and changes. Can you get comments back to me within a week? Is that enough time for you?" I asked.

"No problem," she reassured me.

Somehow saying goodbye to her was easier than with my African friends, Alphonse, Patrick, and others. We hugged, laughed, and told stories as I promised to visit them, at some point in my life. And I knew I would.

I remembered those farewells as Guillermo pulled the taxi to the curb at Juan Santamaria International Airport in San Jose, Costa Rica. The curb was already bustling with American tourists unloading their baggage and surfboards for a vacation in the perfect Pacific Ocean waves of the Nicoya Peninsula. Guillermo unloaded my two large bags, both were filled with treasures and gifts I had accumulated while in Costa Rica for the past year, crafts made by the Ticos and gifts from my African friends.

"*Muchas gracias por todo*, Guillermo." I struggled to say with a lump in my throat and slightly better Spanish than a year ago. I reached out and hugged him tightly and was surprised by the hot tears that welled up in my eyes. This wonderful man had become my go-to taxi driver after I sprained my ankle. Because we spoke different languages, our conversations were elementary as he drove me in his red taxi to my various destinations two or three times a week. But it didn't matter. The language barrier was not a barrier between our hearts. We connected on a deeper level.

I would miss him, too. Again, generosity and love were shining from him, through the strata of life experiences, language barriers, and cultural beliefs, to pierce my heart.

This was what I would take back from Costa Rica. A newly minted master's degree was the original goal, but this deep connection to the human spirit was the true gift I received—the delightfully surprising gift of an open heart and a generous spirit.

Back in San Diego, on July 2, 2005, guests arrived in droves to the welcome home party that Dana planned with such love and commitment. It was another beautiful sunny warm day. The backyard lawn was green and cut to perfection. The rose bushes were in bright bloom with their reds, oranges, yellows, and pinks on full display. The native southern California plants were trimmed, watered, and healthy in this semi-arid climate. Unlike the daily rain of Costa Rica, rain had not fallen in San Diego since April.

I embraced the warm hugs, cards, gifts, and well wishes from my guests, eagerly celebrating my return to San Diego after my year-long adventure in Costa Rica.

And as I expected, I was immediately put on the spot by the question: "What will you do now?" Dana and I had practiced my response the night before, knowing this would be the first question from every person after the hugs and welcome home cheers.

"I will start my own consulting business after I finish my thesis next month," I heard myself say over and over. "In Management Consulting."

"Will you use your peace degree?" my dear friend Jeff, asked. I was delighted to have him join the celebration. We had been through so much together at CSC, and I also feared that on some level he might have felt I abandoned him during my illness—and my retreat to Costa Rica.

"I think my peace degree was for my own peace," I ventured out.

"How so?" he asked.

I shifted my weight from my left leg to my right leg as I contemplated. I wasn't quite ready for this question and found myself in a quandary. Looking into his kind eyes, I decided to trust him with more of my truth, much more than I had shared with him on the elevator incident day.

"I went to Costa Rica to get a master's degree in Peace and International Conflict Studies. I learned about conflict, violence, and war. The need to economically support women, educate children, and protect the environment and natural resources," I paused and was reassured that he was listening intently. "What I didn't expect was that I'd learn so much about myself. How I didn't trust people and how my heart was closed to protect myself from harm. I learned about forgiveness, compassion, and generosity. I don't yet know how to make a living at that, but I want to try it. I can only start with me. So, my personal peace is really what I got from my year in Costa Rica." I was crying again. I was doing that a lot lately.

He reached his arms out to hug me. He was crying, too. "That is beautiful. I wish I could learn that too. We are all working a million hours to make money, earn the next promotion, and get ahead. To what end?" he asked.

"I know. I don't get it. I think we have gotten off track somewhere. I want to keep my new found inner peace, but I am afraid it will get run over by the hustle and bustle of the twisted American dream of success. Do you think it is possible to achieve the dream and maintain peace within oneself?" I asked him with a desperate look.

He simply said, "I hope so. We can't all take a year out of our lives to go to Costa Rica. Help us figure it out, Cindy."

Dear Reader,

Knowledge and wisdom are not meant to be hoarded. They are to be shared. It's time to pay it forward and share your gifts with the world. Your legacy isn't about the wealth acquired, but the wisdom that you can pass on to the generations looking for you to be the leader you truly are when you shine your light in the world.

- *What challenges have you overcome?*
- *What lessons have you learned?*
- *What wisdom can you share with your team, your family, or your community?*

EPILOGUE

IT'S BEEN MORE THAN a dozen years since I graduated from the University for Peace. My growth in body, mind, and spirit continues. I have accepted that we are a work-in-progress, and that everything is a practice, demanding that we continue to learn, resolve any grievances, and be unstoppable. I live my principles and am deeply committed to having fun in all areas of my life—and I do.

And my fun came back! Early in my childhood, I had fun. Then at age eight or nine, it disappeared. Now, I make sure I do everything in my power to have fun everyday—in my personal life and with my clients. I believe we're meant to have fun! And I do. I laugh a lot. Researchers have proven that a good belly laugh bonds people. Try it out sometime! (Principle #1—Tap into Your Fun Quotient!)

My health: I'm dedicated to the disciplines that reestablished my health and well-being. I work out with weights twice a week, do yoga, meditate daily, and sleep 7-8 hours a night. I avoid wheat, sugar, flour, and cows' milk—and alcohol. I gave up alcohol many years ago after a Christmas Day binge in 1990 when I looked into the mirror and saw that I was becoming my father. One phone call later to Alcoholics Anonymous (AA), and I began my journey to sobriety. It's been twenty-seven years. And I'm unstoppable in my sobriety. It wasn't that hard because I chose it—and continue to do so.

Over time, I discovered the source of my health crisis. For years, I had suffered from allergies and sinus infections and took multiple rounds of antibiotics that destroyed my intestinal "good" bacteria that affected the absorption of nutrients into my body. Fundamentally, I was nutritionally starving. This in turn created the environment for an autonomic system dysfunction and the shutdown of my organs.

I overcame my proclivity to "soldiering on," which I discovered was my defense mechanism that kept me from getting too close to friends, family, and colleagues—and prevented me from looking at areas of my life that needed attention.

My commitment and relationship to Dana has strengthened and continues to evolve into a wonderful interdependent dance. I am a better Cindy Henson because I am with Dana Smith. She sees me like no other and keeps me honest, providing a mirror for my self-reflection. Dana retired five years ago and has been perfecting her nature, animal, and bird photography. She backpacks and hikes, and we camp together in Woodstock—our 1969 "canned-ham" travel trailer. She is also the caretaker for her feisty eighty-nine-year-old mother. We celebrated our eighteen-year anniversary this year.

My family: Mom is in her eighties and except for recent knee surgery, she remains in good health. Volunteer work is what brings her joy and she dedicates her time to The American Cancer Society and The American Heart Association. She lives in North Carolina near my sister, Deb.

Deb and Tom, her high school sweetheart, have been married for thirty-seven years. They have two daughters, Jennifer and Jessica who are in their early thirties. Jessica has a son, Landon, who is five. Deb's life revolves around her family, being a confidante for her daughters, and a grandma to Landon. It's what juices her.

Tiffany, Pam's daughter, married her high school sweetheart, Josh. They have three bright and engaged children—Briar, Chase, and Callie, who look like Pam. They reside in Tennessee and are currently building a house.

My friends: I remain in contact with many of my friends from the University for Peace.

Alphonse works for an NGO in Sweden that assists refugees with integrating into the country.

Tory built a prototype/game, started a business, got a grant, pulled a wide team of scholars and local teachers and Native American folks together regarding the Bozeman Trail, an illegal short-cut off the Oregon trail that led to the gold fields in Montana a la Custer *and* modern day standing rock. She developed the scientific methodology to enable implementation to fulfill the Wyoming Indian History curriculum legislative requirement.

After leaving the University for Peace, Muzaffar (Muzy) worked for the Committee to Protect Journalists. He is now working for the Civil Rights Defenders, an independent expert organization founded in Stockholm in 1982 with the aim of defending human rights, in particular people's civil and political rights.

Many others are working or teaching at human rights and peace-oriented foundations, non-profits, and NGOs. When it came down to earning a living, even Adib wanted to work for a corporation. He worked in human resources at Nestlé in the Middle East and is now contributing his talents and enthusiasm at Careem in Dubai.

The Rasur Foundation, the host of the Costa Rica Peace Army, continues with Rita Marie's involvement. The program has evolved to "Be Peace," and has been deployed in Costa Rica and the United States. Those involved in the program continue to teach social and emotional skills for a more connected world. See *Completely Connected: Writing our Empathy and Insights for Extraordinary Results* by Rita Marie Johnson for practical ways to connect to others.

My business is firmly established, and I have successfully combined all that I learned at the University for Peace with my decades of business experience to create a thriving management consulting business. I formed the Henson Consulting Group upon returning from Costa Rica. And even though I am steeped in the business world, I have preserved the knowledge I acquired from my education at UPEACE. I have done what I vowed: I brought the belief system of gentleness and peace to my new private business. Instead of being "corporate," I have incorporated the lessons of the University for Peace into my business, and in doing so, I am influencing many others to embrace the concept of the triple-bottom line and people first.

I work with leaders and organizations that make a positive difference in the world—by definition that is government agencies, non-profits, and triple bottom-line corporations: people, planet, and profit. I partner with other consultants with similar life and people values to fulfill larger contracts. We assist managers and employees to discover their life passion and purpose (CEO^2 designed and licensed) and then bring that to their work life. See *The Accidental CEO* by Tom Voccola and Frances Fujii for more about "The Passion and Purpose Method."

I believe that the one infinite resource that corporations and organizations have is their people, and I assist leaders to empower their employees and create inspired teams by tapping all the talent in the organization, regardless of title or role.

The magic continues. Clients come to me because I provide clarity and alleviate the "loneliness at the top" syndrome that many leaders face. I want to help and they know that, so we work together. Maybe I have become the shining tree.

ACKNOWLEDGMENTS

I AM DEEPLY GRATEFUL for the extraordinary people who helped make this book a reality.

I feel fortunate to have worked with such talented people through much of my life. My early career at Topaz, General Dynamics, GDE Systems, BAE Systems, and Computer Sciences Corporation taught me business analysis, process improvement, project management, leadership and organizational development skills that have been the foundation of my management consulting practice for the last dozen years. The diverse clients and colleagues that I have had the privilege to work with as a consultant have challenged me to perform at a higher level than I previously thought possible, project by project and client by client. You all know who you are so I won't attempt to thank each of you individually. Please know that I am grateful every day to participate with such high caliber human beings that serve employees, customers, and community members in a respectful and meaningful way.

I am blessed to have attended the United Nations University for Peace in Costa Rica as a mature student of forty-six years old. The professors, students, and staff were quality people, with an undying vision and commitment for a peaceful world. I will call out three fellow classmates that I have visited over the past few years who are embodying the peaceful principles we learned at UPEACE.

- **Alphonse**—Thank you for teaching me that generosity is simply a choice. You demonstrate it daily in your refugee integration work. Amazing!

- **Tory**—I appreciate your comradery and your spark that translates to evocative curriculum for our youth. Bravo!
- **Muzy**—Thank you for always speaking your mind and fighting the good fight for free journalism in our world. You go!

While I won't be able to thank everyone, and will inevitably leave people out, please know that I acknowledge from my heart, the support and encouragement many of you provided on this book project. I will name and thank a few key players on Team Cindy.

Eric Klein for introducing me to Jeffrey Davis and "Your Captivating Book Program" in April of 2014.

Jeffrey Davis for showing me the ropes of writing and always being in my corner with encouragement and kind words when I wanted to give up. I have always been an avid reader and did not see myself as a good writer. You moved my skills forward as a writer and now as an author.

Thank you for coalescing such a talented team at Tracking Wonder: **Britt Bravo, Dom John, Erin Hayworth, Holly Moxley,** and **Greg Berg**. Thank you for bringing forward my website, blogs, and social media in support of my business and this book project.

Thank you to Wild Women Writer comrades: **Molly Morrissey, Stephanie Holmes-Farmer, and Suzi Banks-Baum.** I so appreciate our monthly meetings where we read each other our latest writings and received thoughtful encouragement and gentle critique.

Laura Shaine Cunningham for shaping my raw manuscript into a story. When my courage was waning, you told me the story needed to be told. I am grateful to you.

Kathy Sparrow for taking my story and turning it into a compelling read. I appreciate your gift as an editor and a storyteller. You brought my words to life. Thank you for your heartfelt commitment to me and this project.

Justin Sachs and the team at Motivational Press for converting the manuscript into a real book, one that is visually appealing and can be sacredly held in the palm of two hands.

Thank you to the myriad of early readers. You took the time to read the manuscript (some of you several times) and gave important and meaningful feedback that helped shape the book into its final form. Thank you, **Deb Gills, Loli Wescott, Paula Russell, Patricia Branson, Kathy Rosenow, Jim Simon, Dana Smith, Frances Fujii, Eric Klein, Bruce Sindahl, Paula MacKinnon, Georgie Richardson, Len Elder, Tracy Oberlies, Jen Rodrigues, Molly Morrissey, and Karen Lewis.**

Jenny Sudo, my executive assistant, who keeps everything running which allows me to do what I do best, as she does what she does best.

Thank you to my parents, **Bobbie and Harlan Henson** for loving me and imprinting me with my core values of hard work and achievement.

To my sister, **Deb Gills,** thank you for your fun-loving nature, friendship, and unconditional love.

Dana Smith, for stepping in to handle all the household chores and life duties that gave me the space to close myself in my office for nearly every weekend for a year. Thank you for listening to my struggles, vulnerabilities, and doubts as I continued to write. I appreciate your gift of always offering new ways to view situations and circumstances. But I most appreciate that you lovingly and humbly are able to bring me to a new way of thinking. Thank you, my love.

Dear Readers, thank you for going on this journey into the Jungle with me. I appreciate that you trusted me with your time, your mind, and your heart. May you always feel Peace, Purpose, and Freedom in your life.

ABOUT THE AUTHOR

Cynthia L. Henson, the Chief Executive Officer of Henson Consulting Group, is a dynamic leader with deep experience in designing and implementing collaborative and innovative systems to quickly achieve results within large organizations. Cindy brings strong knowledge in developing and executing strategic plans, motivating and directing executive and management teams of employees, suppliers, clients and community citizens across diverse ethnic cultures to achieve stated goals. She also possesses three decades of experience within corporations, local government agencies and non-profits as a business executive and an independent consultant.

She is uniquely qualified to teach and coach executives to their highest level of performance while assisting them in motivating their managers and employees to achieve the desired business outcomes and goals. Cindy has been both a business coach for executives as well as an on-the-ground executive responsible for financials, schedule and performance.

Henson Consulting Group, for which she is the owner and lead consultant, specializes in executive coaching, board development, change management and large-scale project implementation. Cindy has a proven track record at guiding executives to articulate their vision, aligning employees and providing practical tools for successful implementation that is sustainable beyond the Executive Coaching contract.

She is frequently hired to turn-around troubled organizations and projects to bring back financial stability, strengthen teamwork and set clear direction. Her unique set of skills and experiences are rarely found in management consultants. Cindy has extensive experience in leading broad cultural change across large organizations as evidenced in her role as the TQM and Process Improvement Manager for a 3,000-employee division of General Dynamics and as the Director of Organizational Development for the 6,000 person Applications Services Division of Computer Sciences Corporation (CSC).

Cindy has an MBA, with an emphasis in Information Technology and a Masters in International Peace and Conflict Studies from the prestigious United Nations University for Peace. She is also certified by the Society for Human Resource Management (SHRM) as a Senior Professional in Human Resources (SPHR); she is certified in the Myers Briggs Type Indicator (MBTI) and certified in the highly effective tool – Accelerating Change.

Her clientele include: AT&T, General Dynamics, Colibri, RSG, Andrews Lagasse Branch & Bell LLP, Toastmasters International, San Diego Community College District, the University of San Diego, County of San Diego, City of La Quinta, Sunline Transit Agency, the YMCA, the Association for Community Housing Solutions (TACHS), Unity Worldwide Ministries, and many more.

For more information, visit Ms. Henson's website, Henson Consulting Group, www.hensonconsultinggroup.com.